What Now...
I Don't Have Kids!

My Journey Through Infertility
and How I Evolved from Feelings
of Failure to Fulfilment

Sharyn County

First published by Ultimate World Publishing 2025
Copyright © 2025 Sharyn County

ISBN

Paperback: 978-1-923255-21-0
Ebook: 978-1-923255-22-7

Sharyn County has asserted her rights under the Copyright, Designs and Patents Act 1988 to be identified as the author of this work. The information in this book is based on the author's experiences and opinions. The publisher specifically disclaims responsibility for any adverse consequences which may result from use of the information contained herein. Permission to use information has been sought by the author. Any breaches will be rectified in further editions of the book.

All rights reserved. No part of this publication may be reproduced, stored in or introduced into a retrieval system, or transmitted in any form, or by any means (electronic, mechanical, photocopying, recording or otherwise) without the prior written permission of the author. Any person who does any unauthorised act in relation to this publication may be liable to criminal prosecution and civil claims for damages. Enquiries should be made through the publisher.

Cover design: Ultimate World Publishing
Layout and typesetting: Ultimate World Publishing
Editor: Vanessa McKay

Ultimate World Publishing
Diamond Creek,
Victoria Australia 3089
www.writeabook.com.au

Dedication

This book is dedicated to my husband, Al.

It is for all those who have faced infertility at any point in their lives or whose life circumstances have prevented them from having children.

If this book can help one person, then it is a success.

"Sometimes you will never know the value of a moment. Until it becomes a memory."
(Dr Suess)

"The adventure of life is to learn.
The purpose of life is to grow.
The nature of life is to change.
The challenge of life is to overcome.
The essence of life is to care.
The opportunity of life is to serve.
The secret of life is to dare.
The spice of life is to befriend.
The beauty of life is to give."
(William Arthur Ward)

What People Are Saying

Sharyn's journey, so courageously captured in this book, is a profound testament to resilience, authenticity, and the power of vulnerability. Sharyn's story is about the trials of infertility, and about the universal struggle of facing unexpected challenges and redefining one's path in life.

Through her honest reflections, Sharyn has given a voice to those who too often suffer in silence, creating a space of comfort, understanding, and community. The world needs more individuals like Sharyn - brave enough to speak openly about their own struggles and compassionate enough to support others through theirs. Her journey resonates deeply with the mission of the WorldCC Foundation, as both are rooted in a belief that we can and must do so much more in our pursuit of the outcomes of the UN Sustainable Development Goals and in the belief that every individual deserves dignity, support, and the opportunity to live a fulfilling life, no matter the obstacles they face.

I am immensely proud of Sharyn for sharing her story with the world and deeply grateful to call her a friend. This book offers not just solace, but also hope, and a reminder that even when life takes unexpected turns, we can still find joy, purpose, and fulfilment.

Sally Guyer, Global Chief Executive Officer of World Commerce and Contracting, President & CEO of WorldCC Foundation.

Where was this book when I needed it? Sharyn County has penned the essential narrative that the world has needed. Raw, honest, and profoundly real, she courageously shares her journey through IVF, navigating the turbulent waters of infertility with rawness and honesty. 'What Now... I Don't Have Kids' is an exploration of the mental, physical, and emotional toll of longing for motherhood amidst life's unexpected turns. Through personal anecdotes, thought-provoking statistics, and heartfelt insights, Sharyn paints a vivid picture of what is a universal struggle with grace and ease. Having faced five rounds of unsuccessful IVF, I find myself wishing for this book's presence during my own challenging moments. Whether you're a parent or not, Sharyn's narrative will deepen your understanding of the silent battle against infertility and may provide solace for you or someone you know. Sharyn, though you may not wear the title of 'Mum,' you have birthed a legacy of hope, truth, and vulnerability that will resonate with readers for generations to come. Well, done you!
Renée Giarrusso, Founder RG Dynamics and Limitless Leadership. International Award-Winning Author, Master Trainer, Keynote Speaker and Coach.

This is a powerful book capturing one inspiring woman's journey through infertility, and coming to terms with childlessness - both of which are taboo topics. Sharyn shares brave insight into her experience of fertility treatment and navigating childlessness. She approaches the topics with openness, vulnerability, and sometimes humour. Sharyn also explores the societal expectations of motherhood and the challenges she has faced, and continues to face, in a pro-natal society. Crucially, she conveys a message of hope and inspiration, shining a light on alternative paths to fulfilment – the Plan B we seldom hear about…

**Katy Schnitzler,
Academic and Founder of MIST Workshops Ltd.**

Sharyn has written such a vulnerable, brave and incredibly well researched book sharing her own experience of infertility, with insights gained from a diagnosis of PCOS, the societal perceptions of infertility, and how they impact a person's experience.

This book is so powerful, covering the ripple effect on all aspects of a person's life, from relationships with family and friends to how it impacts the workplace. It sets out a clear picture of how infertility takes a hold on all aspects of a person's life. What I love about how Sharyn's approach is both the honesty she shares about her own feelings from failure and sadness to the positivity and acceptance she has learnt to incorporate in her life formed from her and her partner's resilience - against all odds.

'What Now… I Don't Have Kids' is a fascinating read for anyone personally dealing with the huge emotional toll of trying to conceive and how to process their grief that comes with not getting the positive outcome so often portrayed with the narrative around ART (Assisted Reproductive Technology). It is evidence based and has such a compassionate tone with the accompanying tips on how to come to terms with the acceptance of what life looks like without kids. I think it will be a huge help for anyone grappling with infertility, as well as being a brilliant resource for the workplace to be more mindful and empathetic to the childless, not-by-choice community.

Natalie Silverman, Co-Founder & CCO of Fertility Matters at Work and Founder of The Fertility Podcast.

Sharyn County courageously acts as our social conscience about the unspoken – infertility – and its wide-reaching impact. Sharing her butterfly moment, she reminds us of the power of hope, growth and resilience.

Penny Sahinis, Director, Strategic HR & Advisory Services of G.A.P Management Consulting.

I first met Sharyn in contracting and procurement, where her leadership and wisdom highlighted the need for a more optimistic mindset to navigate complex challenges. In *What Now... I Don't Have Kids*, Sharyn brings that same clarity, courage, and optimism to one of life's most personal and arduous journeys. Sharyn tries to be an eternal optimist no matter the circumstances, and her message to us is clear: choose to be optimistic and embrace life. Her story is a powerful reminder that despite grief and unfulfilled dreams, there is still hope, growth, and joy. This book is a testament to optimism as the underpinning of resilience and the strength of the human spirit.

Victor Perton ('That Optimism Man'), CEO and Chief Optimism Officer of The Centre for Optimism.

Disclaimer

This book may trigger painful memories or current painful experiences. Please seek help if this occurs.

This book is not intended as a substitute for advice provided by a doctor or other healthcare professionals.

The content within this book is my personal story, and the expressions and opinions are based on actual life events. In telling this story, I recount my own experiences. I do not presume to tell the story of others who feature in this book. The feelings, thoughts, and memories expressed are mine, and this is my perspective alone.

This reflects my experience and may not represent the experiences of others, as every journey will be unique.

Despite best efforts, this book may still contain some inaccuracies, including statistics, data, and information related to the world of ART (Assisted Reproductive Technology). I have drawn on my research and experience as part of my story to assist in setting the scene for my journey. Data and information are collected in different ways within this field, and there can be significant variation. Therefore, it is important to seek medical advice and do your own research based on your unique circumstances.

The material in this book consists of general comments only and does not purport or intend to be advice. Readers should not act on the basis of any material in this book without seeking professional advice regarding their own individual circumstances. The author expressly disclaims all and any liability to any person, whether or not they purchased this book, in respect of anything and the consequences of anything done or omitted to be done by any such person in reliance, whether whole or partial, upon the whole or any part of the contents of this book.

Please seek help if you need it.

Contents

Dedication	iii
What People Are Saying	v
Disclaimer	ix
Foreword	xiii
INTRODUCTION: My Why	1
ONE: This Is Me	11
Polycystic Ovary Syndrome (PCOS)	21
TWO: What The… Infertility	25
Age and Infertility	31
Assisted Reproductive Technology (ART) Treatment	34
The Statistics	36
THREE: The Cycles Of Disappointment	41
Available Information	45
The IVF Cycle of Disappointment	47
The Devastating Impact of COVID-19	51
FOUR: Feeling Stuck Inside Our Cocoon	55
Grief	58
Deciding to Stop	66
FIVE: You Are Not Alone	73
Our Support	78

SIX: Don't Forget Your Lippy 91
    The Things People Say 94
    The Loss We Felt 100
    Managing Baby Showers and Other Triggers 102

SEVEN: We Bought A Boat! 107

EIGHT: Breaking Free From Our Cocoon 117
    How Others Feel 122
    Ongoing Grief 127

NINE: Embrace The Raindrops 131
    Creating My Purpose 137
    Being Grateful Everyday 139

TEN: Why Don't We Talk About It? 143
    Workplace Challenges 147

ELEVEN: What Next… 161
    Illness 163
    Being Grandparents 165
    Aging Without Children 166

TWELVE: Evolutionary Insights 169

Afterword 177

Acknowledgements 179

About the Author 181

References 183

Foreword

I believe you need to let go of your preconceptions about who you thought you would be and accept the new you. The person you are meant to be.

I have used a butterfly image to represent my transition. From feeling like a failure, cocooned in darkness and feeling as though my life had not yet begun, much like the caterpillar, to eventually evolving like a butterfly and discovering fulfilment despite not having the children I desired.

Even at the end of a journey that you did not plan for, you can still transform into something beautiful that brings joy to both yourself and others. Butterflies teach us that something wonderful awaits at the end of a gruelling journey. For me, a butterfly stands for hope, change and happiness. They were also my Nan's favourite creatures, so I smile and think of her whenever I see one.

> *"Just when the caterpillar thought the world was over, it became a butterfly."*
> ***(Zhuangzi - Chuang Tzu)***

INTRODUCTION

My Why

"The two most important days in your life are the day you are born and the day you find out why."
(Mark Twain)

I am infertile. My husband Al and I do not have kids, and we have experienced grief and heartache throughout the rollercoaster process of trying to have them. This is my journey but also the journey I travelled with Al, so sometimes I refer to us ("we"), not just myself.

I am not an expert. We are just regular people who have gone through this experience. This book aims to share our experiences, hopefully helping others feel less alone, and it serves as a tool for our ongoing healing, ensuring this does not continue to define who I am or who we are as a couple. This is the story about how we got off the rollercoaster of fertility treatments, stopped focusing on getting pregnant, got our life back, and focused on living our lives to the fullest.

According to the World Health Organisation (WHO), it is a human right for anyone to have a child if they choose to.[1] Therefore, it is fundamentally important that there is a greater focus on infertility, whether that is biological or circumstantial. We need to support those in our society who have not been fortunate enough to experience that human right and show them that life can still be just as fulfilling.

Infertility is a disease[2] that is significantly prevalent across the globe,[3] and its treatments have implications greater than the inability to conceive. A journey through the uncertainty of infertility brings a multitude of consequences that can impact not only the individual but also the families and societies around them. These consequences can include physical, psychological, and financial impacts. How this plays out for individuals can vary depending on their location, and where they live can influence the type of challenges those individuals may face. I want more people to understand this disease and recognise that it affects many people around the world and is not something you can easily 'get over.'

Being in Australia, we are extremely lucky to live in a country where the treatments and systems around us are strong. Although there is room for improvement, we at least had access to various treatments and had the opportunity and financial means to try to have children. There are so many who do not get that opportunity. We also had each other. For me, I had a supportive and loving husband, family, and friends who did not judge me for being unable to be a mum or for not enabling Al to be a dad.

We need to ensure that everyone, regardless of their location and no matter who they are, their gender, their choice of partner or their choice to be on their own, can have access to all the things necessary to enable them to have children, should they wish to.

This book is not about how to be successful with IVF; rather, it details our infertility journey, which included an unsuccessful IVF process marked by an endless cycle of disappointment. It explores how we came to terms with this and how we got to the end of this journey. Importantly, it reflects on how we navigated this disappointing, agonising and heartbreaking experience and how other aspects of our lives have enabled us to find fulfilment and happiness. My aim in writing this book has been to provide an honest account of the challenges we faced along the way. It also touches on how those around us felt during this time, as well as the perspectives of others who faced obstacles that kept them from becoming parents.

The journey of writing this book was a means for me to finalise and provide meaning to this part of my life while also helping and supporting others. My hope is that readers will understand they can be okay even if IVF, or any other fertility treatment, does not work for them or if life circumstances have prevented them from becoming a parent.

While there are many books, shows and podcasts that talk about the struggle of infertility, they commonly focus on positive outcomes. Through this book, I wanted to share my experience with infertility and not becoming a parent in order to help those who are grappling with childlessness or those who are navigating their own journeys and trying to understand the implications if they are unsuccessful.

Furthermore, many books tell you how to get pregnant, what to do when you are pregnant, and how to raise your children. There are few that address what to do when, due to circumstances, you are not a parent and how to cope with and manage an outcome you had not anticipated.

This book is also something I would have liked when we were in the middle and at the end of our journey. To hear that others were on the same path as us and to see that we would be okay and would emerge stronger with fulfilment and joy in our lives would have helped me immensely.

Regardless of our challenges, we choose to be optimistic and embrace life.

Our experience has taught us a lot, and we have become incredibly resilient. While the pain never goes away, we are still living a rewarding life, though different from how we imagined it to be. This book was written for anyone who is in the middle of this journey, who is at the start or at the end and who has thought that there is no life beyond parenthood or that you are the only one. It's about what worked for us and continues to work for us. It is about how we figured out what helped during, and at the end of this - to put it bluntly - crappy cycle of disappointment!

Being infertile is a very lonely process. It is challenging and full of grief, sadness and heartache where you feel there is no end. But, it is your choice how you move on from this process. It is you who has the power to move forward, embrace the life you have been given and live it to its fullest. This journey is filled with disappointment, failure, and grief, but you can also have laughs along the way. Everyone deals with disappointment, failure, and grief in their own way and it is okay to remain optimistic and find humour, even through the toughest times.

Your journey through infertility will differ from ours and many others, but we have some common ground and can truly empathise with each other and support each other when and where we need to. I resonate with how Brené Brown, on a YouTube clip I watched, summed up empathy as the process of showing someone that you know what it is like to be in their situation and letting them see they are not alone.[4]

> *"Empathy fuels connection.*
> *Sympathy drives disconnection."*[5]
> **(Dr. Brené Brown, 2013)**

Our experience has enabled me to empathise with others going through a similar process. Throughout my career, I have met, supported, and led people who were going through their journey and dealing with some form of infertility. While everyone's circumstances are different, there is one common theme: we feel or felt alone. We have felt like failures, we have felt ashamed to tell others, and we felt as though we were the only ones going through this.

You are not alone.

Given the prevalence of infertility, there will be many individuals in our workplaces who may be or may have experienced infertility, with many navigating fertility treatment in secret. I do not understand why topics associated with fertility are not discussed more openly. Including why we don't talk about being pregnant or trying to be pregnant until after 12 weeks gestation. If you are struggling or have a loss, you need others to understand what is happening and give you (and your partner) the support needed. Why are these subjects still taboo to discuss even now?

For me, it's vital that we have open discussions with family, friends, and work colleagues around these topics. We need to be able to help people throughout their process and support them in their careers while navigating these challenging times. People affected by these experiences deserve to be given the support they need.

While we can't control all circumstances, we can choose how they shape our identity and influence our lives.

Whether it's infertility, life circumstances, illness in you or your family, mental health, career challenges, menopause, period issues, death of someone close or losing a child, all these things and many more can impact how you bring yourself to life and work. It's essential we talk about these rather than hold up a life of such a high standard. We need to be open about this to let others know they will be okay, that life goes on, and that we will get through what seems, at times like the toughest moments in our life, only happens to us.

As a woman focused on her career, I see many women talking about 'having it all' - the distinguished career, the large family, the work-life balance. I also want to let people know it is okay if you do not get it all, and not everyone does. We need to talk more about our challenges rather than continuously focus on the fairy tale. If all we see are those who apparently 'have it all,' then we start to feel less worthy and feel more like failures when we have struggles. It's important we show that not everyone has it all and that social media and the pressure of appearing as though you have it all does not help those who are struggling.

From puberty to periods, to fertility to menopause, we need to talk about it, and we need to be okay about having those discussions. My wish is that we make these conversations around what have long been perceived as taboo subjects part of regular everyday conversations and create a safe space for people through their various phases of life.

As a woman, a stigma exists in which assumptions are made that you are not a mum because you are focused on your career or you are selfish. Everyone's journey is different, whether due to circumstances, infertility, illness, or even choice. We need to stop judging others or putting unrealistic expectations on people to conform. We also need to figure out how we make our policies and initiatives focus on ALL rather than just those who are lucky enough to be or want to become parents.

While we have grieved and were unsuccessful and felt like a failure and all alone, we continue to lean into a fulfilling and balanced life, even if it differs from what we had initially anticipated. Though you may not see it or feel it now, you will be okay, and it does not make you less of a person if you are not a parent. Not being parents is, and will not be, the only adversity we face together. Life will continue to throw more challenges at you, which is part of life. We cannot control everything, but we can control how we let these situations define who we are and how we let them take over our lives.

Embrace the life you've got. Don't waste it worrying about the things you don't have or can't control.

The most significant learning curve for me was to embrace life again. I could not waste my life worrying about what we did not have or was out of our control. Instead, we appreciate what we have and the joyful moments we experience and embrace them all. My husband and I have come out of this process much stronger within ourselves and our relationship. And now, despite our challenges, we choose to remain optimistic and embrace the life we have. We can get through anything now, and boy, does life continue to challenge us!

I try to be an eternal optimist no matter the circumstances. However, this has been challenging, to say the least.

My why for writing this book is to help others going through similar journeys. Even if only one person resonates with my journey and it helps them through theirs, then my why will have been fulfilled.

Everyone's story is their story. This is mine from my perspective.

> *"Failure is just a sign that we need to widen our scope. We need to be ready and build ourselves up for the next level. Actually, what we end up achieving is far greater than what we'd envisioned for ourselves."* [6]
> **(*Jay Shetty, 2016*)**

ONE

This Is Me

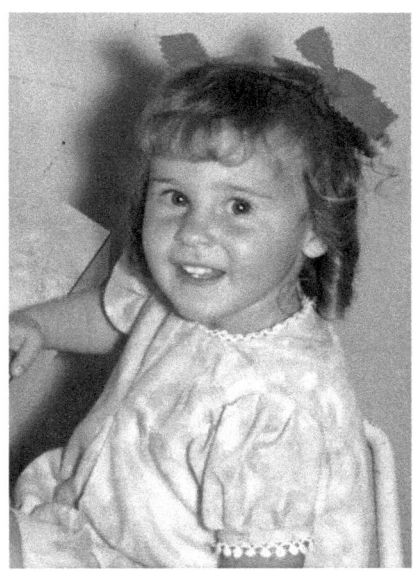

*"In the end, just three things matter:
How well we have lived.
How well we have loved.
How well we have learned to let go."[7]*
(Jack Kornfield, 1994)

What I told myself
Kids will be a big part of my life.
I want a loud and vibrant house with lots of kids running around.
When the time is right, I will be a mum.
Becoming a mum will be easy. Everyone does it!
There shouldn't be any issues for us. Why would there be?

It was early 2008, leading into my 40th birthday, and my body was in a good space to try another cycle. This could be it. This could be the one. We were excited (but tried not to get too excited given all the letdowns we had experienced previously). We had talked about ending this cycle of disappointment once I hit 40, and we had come to terms with this being the final go.

But we were sure it would work this time. How could it not? Why would it not? What could be wrong with us? Why would we be the only ones not able to do this? Everyone else does it so easily! What could we have done to deserve this? How come this is happening to us? Don't let yourself get too excited, given it has failed every other time.

This was a time of mixed emotions, trying to be positive but always disappointed and let down.

> *"Where there is hope, there is life. It fills us with fresh courage and makes us strong again."*[8]
> **(Anne Frank, 1947)**

Failure!
I could not get just one egg!

That was it!

No more trying. We had to let it go!

How can we let it go?

What if the next one was it?

Maybe just one more try?

We had to stop this and move on; this last one was not the one, and we had had enough. 40 was my end point, and I did not want to go into my 40s still trying to get something we may never have. It was easy to get caught up in the pursuit of it rather than set an end point and focus on the 'what now?' and what our life could be. Finding an endpoint for our journey and having this as the deadline helped us stop and refocus our lives.

The grief associated with our fertility struggles and the intangible grief related to its lack of success was overwhelming and extremely hard to navigate. We wanted our lives back and to stop feeling so sad all the time. It was time to face reality, to embrace and celebrate what we had and not dwell on what we may never get.

It was devastating. I was in SHOCK.

Our life, like many others, had difficulties with various losses of loved ones and friends along the way. This was hard, and we grieved through these times as you grieve for the loss of those you love. Our relationship and marriage felt effortless and blessed, and the life we created together was fun, carefree, and easy before we started trying to have a family of our own.

I was born in the late 60s, and growing up, I had a clear vision of what my life would be like at an early age.

My childhood was stable with mum, dad, two sisters and a brother. We always had many people around us growing up. Cousins and friends were always close by. Mum and Dad are still together, and all four grandparents remained together until they passed; they all lived to their late 80s and 90s. Having a large and loud family with friends around is important. I wanted a home that was loud and filled with lots of people and lots of activity. Al wanted this as well.

Growing up in the 80s was both fun and carefree. We enjoyed the best fashion, music, and hairstyles, and I see some of these trends are now making a comeback. Let's hope the frizzy perms or Farrah Fawcett Flip do not make their way back! During my early years, we had a lot of fun road trips, with all of us cramped into the Valiant station wagon, fighting, laughing, and annoying each other along the way.

My siblings and I are only two years apart, so we shared many childhood memories and had a lot of fun. I wished for the same experience with a car full of crazy kids, laughing and having fun on road trips. Broken windshields, wearing ski goggles to stop the wind, packing too many shoes, packing the wrong clothes, wearing too many t-shirts, bloody noses and adventures while trying to go to the bathroom on the side of the road (there is a story with a prickle bush but not for this book!). That was the 70s and 80s, and some great memories for me. Holidays were simple, and life was not too complicated.

I smile when recalling childhood memories and stuff we did as kids. One memory that has stayed with me includes all four of us kids packing our suitcases on a trip to Mildura and running away together from the caravan park we were staying at (I cannot recall why). I remember we circled the block hand in hand for what seemed like hours because we could not cross the road. It gives me joy today when I think of this time.

> ***I assumed that when the time was right, I would meet the right person and just be a mum.***

We had many big family get-togethers with everyone: grandparents, aunties, uncles, and cousins. It was wild, loud and a whole lot of fun. I wanted this with a family of my own and assumed I would get it as everyone just did. Didn't they? I loved this time. I wanted to grow up, meet the right person, buy a house, and become a mum.

Two out of three isn't bad.

From age 15, I worked part-time and enjoyed the money and independence this gave me. At the end of school and before university, I worked in childcare, reiterating my desire to be a mum at some point in my life. But I was not ready then and needed to explore other things. I travelled the world and Australia. I worked and studied hard. I assumed I would meet the right person and be a mum when the time was right. It never crossed my mind that this would not happen to me. I almost took this for granted and never considered age or circumstances an issue. Everyone else did it easily, right? In fact, one of my sisters had twins and then another one. My other sister had a girl, a boy, and a stepdaughter, and my brother has five now. I assumed this would be my journey.

There was no reason why it would not be. Most of us grow up thinking we would become a mum or a parent—especially my generation—and it never crossed my mind that I would have any difficulty in conceiving.

Travel has always been a big part of my life, and during my 20s and early 30s, I travelled the world. I saw amazing places, met amazing people, and had once-in-a-lifetime experiences (that's another book I might write). I lived in London and Perth. I met many people along the way and had many incredible adventures in many countries, including the UK, Europe, the Middle East, South America, Africa, and Asia. I felt free and invincible during this time and lived life to the full. I would not swap this for anything, as it made me who I am today. I had partners along the way, and each one taught me something. While I did not end up with any of them, I built (and still have) several lifelong friends from these relationships.

I have been blessed with a wonderful life, a great family, amazing friends, and unforgettable adventures. Through all this, at some point, I just assumed I would still have the family and experiences I had as a kid. You never think there could be problems because you have never really heard about the challenges others face when trying to conceive. Society didn't, and still doesn't talk about it.

When I finally settled back in Melbourne, I was in my early 30s and had already lived a big life. I bought my first place, an apartment only a short walk to the nearest pub and felt independent and in control. This was life. I felt content. With this blessed life, all my struggles to this point were just lessons to be learnt and were all worth going through and gave me life experiences.

It was at this point when I was in the right place with myself I met Al, the love of my life. We met across a crowded pub (cliché but true!). He is a wonderful human, and I knew right away I would marry him, even if it took him a little bit longer to realise we were meant to be together (I put this down to him being 5 years younger than me!). I always wanted kids, and so did he. We had both had adventurous lives leading up to our meeting and were now ready for the next chapter. It was fast, fun, and destined. We were engaged within 12 months and married within two years.

Our wedding was amazing. Everyone probably thinks that about their wedding, but this really was. It was fun and full of laughs. We celebrated into the night and shared our love for each other with family and friends. During the wedding speeches, my friends reminisced about my childhood and mentioned that all I wanted was to be a mum - one of them even said I wanted five kids! I cannot recall telling them this, but I must have said it at some point.

Before we got married and before we started to try to conceive, we discovered a genetic disorder in Al's family, and we needed to determine if I was a carrier of this genetic disorder as well. Al had been recently diagnosed as a carrier, and if both of us were, there was a high chance we would pass the disorder onto our children. This meant we would need to conceive via IVF to undergo embryo tests to rule out the issue. This was the beginning of discussing IVF. We needed to get this cleared up.

Thankfully, we were told that all was good. I was not a carrier, so we could continue our journey to conceive naturally. It was going to happen for us, we didn't need to worry...

Or so we thought!

At the end of this process, I did not think I would end up going through IVF anyway.

I was almost 33 when we married, and we wanted to start a family immediately, so farewell to all contraception methods and smoking. Hello, weight gain which was impacted by quitting smoking and what I did not know at the time - Polycystic Ovary Syndrome (PCOS) - a common hormonal disorder (please refer p.21 for more information). What I then discovered was that PCOS was also going to affect my chances of being able to fall pregnant as well as being 'overweight,' and so began my journey of diet and exercise to try to manage the unmanageable. PCOS also has a counter effect on you - the more you try to lose weight, the more you seem to put on. Add to this the stress of infertility and all the hormones you are adding to your body, and there is no way you can manage this effectively.

So begins the cycle of self-loathing and disappointment.

> **Infertility impacts everyone equally, irrespective of gender or circumstance.**

From an early age, I remember experiencing issues with my period - they were painful and inconsistent. My doctor at the time suggested that I go on the contraceptive pill to help address the problems. There was no information or knowledge provided to me about what this could mean, and little was known, let alone spoken, about infertility as a potential issue. The pill made me regular, and all the other problems disappeared. I had been on the pill since I was 16, and this had masked the hormonal issues I had and any potential challenges I would face trying to conceive in the future.

Growing up in the 80s, my generation did not talk about fertility or possible fertility issues associated with menstruation, so I did not know I would end up where I was. Thankfully, now, we have Fertility Matters, a group founded by the first Australian IVF baby and one of the first-generation IVF babies from the UK, which campaigns for fertility health awareness.[9] Fertility Matters wants everyone to be able to talk about fertility health and to feel empowered. They have developed several educational programmes aimed at educating the younger generation on fertility health to enable them to have more informed discussions and, therefore, make more informed decisions. Unfortunately, I did not know I had issues until I was in my 30s and stopped taking the pill. Having educational programmes like this may have helped me to ensure I focused on my body and how it operated at an early age rather than just masking the issues I had by taking the pill.

These programmes will assist many girls and women in understanding their menstrual cycles and how this could impact their chances of becoming pregnant. They will help to demystify the disease of infertility while reducing the stigma and taboo around the discussions on this topic. If I had known earlier that something was going to impact my fertility, I might have taken steps to minimise this and preserve my chances of being a mum. When I was younger, this never crossed my mind because we never spoke about fertility at all; we just focused on trying not to fall pregnant.

If I had been more informed, it may have helped diminish some of the pain, guilt, and self-blame I felt during our process of trying to conceive. There is a need for a lot more awareness about fertility and how it can or cannot be improved. We need to make sure everyone understands their fertility status so they can potentially mitigate any future issues through lifestyle changes, freezing eggs when young or not waiting for the perfect moment and missing the opportunity. Being fully informed would enable people to know and understand what their choices are and what their chances are going to be. I wish I had known more and I had known earlier. Maybe I would not have done things differently, but what it would have done for me was to have taken away the stigma, the feeling of failure, and the feeling that it was all me. I could have gone into my journey knowing that my chances were slim or that we may not succeed.

Twenty years ago, no one understood much about these issues, and the advice given was contradictory. My ultimate diagnosis of PCOS was not that well understood. And it was not until we were trying to get pregnant that I was even diagnosed. While it is important to talk about PCOS for context in this book, I will not delve into the subject too deeply. Today, there is a lot of research and information you can easily find on this topic, substantially more than when I was diagnosed, but I will describe some aspects of it and the issues I was dealing with during my journey.

> **You spend the majority of your younger years doing everything you can to avoid falling pregnant.**

Polycystic Ovary Syndrome (PCOS)

PCOS is a hormonal disorder that affects 1 in 10 women of reproductive age, according to Jean Hailes for Women's Health, this makes it one of the most common hormonal conditions affecting women.[10]

PCOS is a syndrome with various symptoms, which can differ from person to person, and each symptom has a different associated issue - some people have a few, and some people have them all. The level of androgens (male hormones) you have in your body is increased, resulting in some people having excessive body hair; your body can be insulin resistant in which your body makes insulin but cannot process it effectively; you carry excess weight; and/or you can have inconsistent ovulation resulting in irregular periods, or none at all, as eggs do not regularly form.[11] There is also the condition of Polycystic Ovaries, in which you have cysts on your ovaries, but this is different to the syndrome PCOS.[12]

For me, I had the type of PCOS that included issues with insulin resistance, irregular periods, and minimal ovulation.

As outlined earlier, women with PCOS experience a variety of symptoms and, as such, can have different fertility issues. However, I recall that when I received my diagnosis, the first thing I was told was that I would never be able to conceive naturally, and this was said to most women I spoke to during this time. It felt like there was no widespread understanding of the condition.

Today, with all the information and research available, we now know that even with PCOS, you can still naturally conceive, and there have been women I know who have done precisely that. However, most still needed some level of assistance, whether that was through lifestyle changes, medication, or fertility treatment. Unfortunately, even with all the information available, there is still no apparent reason why someone gets PCOS, and there is still no cure for this condition. There has been some research that suggests that lifestyle and genetics are factors that play a role in PCOS, and having a better understanding of this condition early in life may provide an opportunity to reduce the symptoms and improve fertility.[13]

PCOS brought several issues for me, especially when I stopped taking the pill - my weight exploded due to the insulin resistance aspects of the syndrome, and my menstruation was erratic. My periods were extremely heavy (not fun while out and about), and sometimes I would go months without one. This was an issue while trying to conceive because you constantly thought you were pregnant when you clearly were not. I cannot tell you how many tests I did when I went off the pill, thinking I was late and maybe pregnant, but this was not the case. It was my PCOS that caused my irregular ovulation and menstruation. It was heartbreaking.

It was one disappointment after another.

We thought getting pregnant would be easy - go off the pill and Bam! After all, that happened to everyone else, didn't it? And it is very ironic as you spend most of your younger years doing everything possible not to fall pregnant as you always assumed it would happen easily when you were ready.

We never thought we would come out of this without kids.

We have grieved and continue to grieve for not having children, as well as everything that comes with that. However, I am grateful for what we have and for all we have accomplished, and I am finally at peace now that our life has taken a different path than the one we had planned.

My Top 5 Evolutionary Insights

1. Family, friends, and life experiences are the essence of living and what life is truly about.
2. What you think or plan will happen may never happen. Plans can and will continuously change. Be prepared.
3. What seems easy for many may not be easy for all.
4. Start thinking about a backup plan. Have a plan B.
5. Educate yourself about your body and how it works.

"Do not judge me by my success, judge me by how many times I fell down and got back up again."
(Nelson Mandela)

TWO

What The... Infertility

*"I can be changed by what happens to me.
But I refuse to be reduced by it."*
(Maya Angelou)

What I told myself
What do you mean I have a fertility issue?
What the… how did this happen to me?
What did I do to cause this?
How can I fix it?
Surely, I can fix it? Can't I?
This was not in the plan!
What do I do now?

In 2018, ten years after we stopped our IVF process, the World Health Organisation (WHO) recognised infertility as a disease defined as the failure to achieve a pregnancy after twelve months of regular unprotected sexual intercourse.[14] The fact that the WHO now recognises infertility as a disease stirs up complex emotions within me, as it finally provides a label for the issues I have faced and affirms that it is not something I have caused. However, it also makes me feel upset that infertility hadn't been recognised and a definition did not exist when I went through my personal struggles with it all those years ago.

Thankfully, we are seeing a greater emphasis on infertility, with the WHO having a particular focus on ensuring that everyone has the right, specifically an **essential** human right, to have a child if they wish to, regardless of gender, race, or location.[15] Additionally, having infertility could take away this essential human right from individuals and diminish their lives.[16] This focus will benefit many, as it is likely to drive more significant conversations, greater financial and emotional support, increased availability of services and information, greater data transparency, and additional global research.

> **1 in 6 individuals globally have been affected by the inability to have a child at some point in their life.**

When infertility was officially recognised as a disease in 2018, the WHO estimated that somewhere between **48 million couples and 186 million individuals lived with infertility across the globe.**[17] Today, it is astoundingly estimated that as many as **1 in 6 individuals** will have been impacted or will be impacted by infertility **globally** during their lifetime, significantly impacting their ability to have a child.[18] This estimate was part of a groundbreaking WHO report called Infertility Prevalence Estimates 1990-2021 ('The WHO report'), released in April 2023. The report also aimed to address the issues faced by those suffering with infertility. In research conducted in Australia, the statistics are aligned with the WHO estimate, suggesting that 1 in 6 couples in Australia and New Zealand also suffer infertility.[19] To put the statistics into perspective, if there were **20 people of reproductive age in a Boardroom, 3 would have a fertility issue.**

The WHO report was developed to define and assess global infertility data, but it is also aiming to achieve much more than that. It advocates the establishment of a universal infertility definition and consistent measurement methodology that can be used globally. Doing this enables a broader understanding of the issues associated with infertility that can have widespread consequences for individuals and their communities. These consequences span both physical and mental health implications, financial distress, and the social stigma that can escalate to domestic violence. Additionally, it may help widen the infertility dialogue, which still concentrates predominantly on women, even though male factors also play a significant role.

The WHO report has been, and continues to be, revolutionary because it shows that the issue of infertility is global and one that desperately needs to be addressed. We need to enable everyone to have access to reliable, affordable, and obtainable treatments, regardless of their individual circumstances, gender or family dynamics, and we need to develop policies and practices to support this. The WHO is taking the lead in calling for universal access to affordable, high-quality fertility care and improved fertility clinic results and treatment data for meaningful outcomes and programmes. The WHO is also linking the need to address infertility with the need to meet the United Nations Sustainable Development Goals (UN SDGs), specifically the goals of good health and well-being for all and gender equality.[20]

This focus from the WHO is critical for anyone going through this journey as it will not only help push governments around the globe to ensure fertility treatments are a fundamental human right, but also to help make treatments accessible and affordable to all. However, despite growing discussions, The WHO report indicates that infertility still remains underrepresented globally, with limited focus and limited resources dedicated to it in many parts of the world.

Given this finding, we need to recognise that the implications of infertility and its treatments can actually be far greater than the inability to conceive. Unfortunately, in certain regions globally, societal pressures on fertility can stigmatise individuals who are unable to conceive and have children, so it seems that the variation of how this plays out for each individual can be based on where they are in the world - and this should not be the case. For us, we had access to services and treatments and the financial and emotional support to enable us to undertake the process of assisted reproductive therapies. I am incredibly grateful that we were at least given this opportunity, and I got to share the process with a supportive partner.

Infertility is a disease that can take its toll, leading to anxiety and depression, which can have serious ramifications for a person's mental health and psychosocial well-being. Because of this, it can also lead to an increased risk of intimate partner violence. This isn't a modern phenomenon either. If we go back to Henry the 8th and his documented issues with having a son (which now some say was attributed to his own fertility issues), the ramifications on his wives were significant.[21]

Recent research suggests that there is a link between increased risk of Intimate Partner Violence (IPV), either physical, psychological, emotional or financial, and infertility. It revealed that IPV against infertile women in some countries was as high as 47.2% over a lifetime, with psychological violence being the most common form, followed by physical, sexual, and then economic coercion.[22] This is significantly higher than the estimated 30% of women who experience IPV not explicitly linked to fertility worldwide[23] or 21% of women in Australia.[24] While more research is needed to truly understand the prevalence of infertility-related IPV, it highlights the vulnerability of women who are infertile and the need to have support systems in place to help these women, as these statistics are frightening.

This prevalence of stigma, violence, and lack of support faced by women who have infertility requires urgent attention, so these issues that affect many areas of society can be addressed.

This, coupled with the WHO report, should surely highlight the urgency.

> **If you are struggling and feel alone, I want to remind you are not alone.**

Given the prevalence and challenges of infertility outlined above, I find it astounding that we don't talk about infertility more. But with the work the WHO and others are doing, I am hopeful that this will no longer be a taboo subject, and with an increase in more transparent discussions, those who have infertility will not feel so alone.

While the numbers of those who are infertile seem significant enough, they don't, however, cover circumstantial infertility. This is infertility, not through choice. This is where people are prevented from being able to conceive or attempting to conceive because, for example, they are in same-sex relationships, are single, have physical illness, or have age-related issues. The call to have a broader definition of infertility is critical for those with circumstantial infertility, especially given the WHO outlines that it is an essential human right for anyone to have a child if they wish to.

It is also hopeful that the spotlight from the WHO will enable greater focus on achieving the UN SDGs and helping many people around the world become parents, regardless of their circumstances.

Age and Infertility

There have been articles and discussions recently indicating that the prevalence of infertility is also closely associated with people having babies later in life. We are seeing a drop in fertility and birth rates across the globe, with a fall from an average of 5 births per woman in 1950 to only 2.3 births per woman in 2021, and it is predicted that this rate will drop even further to 2.1 by 2050. 2.1 is the number needed to maintain population levels; however, this is an average figure. There are some regions in the globe where this figure is higher, but also some regions where this figure is significantly lower.[25] If we look at Australia rather than globally, we see that this figure has been falling significantly and well below 2.1 since the 1960s.[26] In 1961, there were 3.55 babies per woman, compared to just 1.7 in 2021. In the last 30 years, we have seen a shift in the age of women giving birth with a considerable decline in how many babies were born per 1000 women between 1990 and 2021 within the age range of 20-24 compared to the increase within the age range of 35-39.[27]

Age	1990 Babies Born	2021 Babies Born
15-19	22.1	7.1
20-24	79.4	38.8
35-39	34.7	70.9
40-44	5.5	15.6

(Source: Australian Bureau of Statistics Website, Births Australia, 2021 | Australian Bureau of Statistics (abs.gov.au))

In addition, the median age of mothers has shifted from 28.33 years in 1990 to 31.7 years in 2021.[28] This shift could be attributed to women having more options and individual circumstances, including choosing to have children later in life due to career, meeting a partner later, social/financial reasons, or not at all.

What these statistics show is that there is more support needed for those having children later in life, given age is a factor in infertility. This correlation between fertility and age is supported by numerous research studies that have explored the relationship between female age and fertility. It is frequently documented that female fertility declines rapidly from the age of 30, and I was 34 when we started our journey. The data shows that the monthly chance of natural conception decreases from 20% around the age of 30 down to 5% for those over 40.[29] Interestingly, this is not just an issue for women but also men, as they have seen a greater risk of miscarriage when men are over 45.[30] Another factor impacting the ability to conceive is that the fertility window in women is small - it is only from 5 days before ovulation to the day of ovulation (if you ovulate at all).[31]

So… the odds were against us from the start.

Our journey began when I went off the pill. My menstruation cycle was all over the place; I could go for months without one, and then when I got it, it would be horrific and unexpected. This was not fun, and I certainly did not wear white during this time. When I was going through all this, there weren't all the high-tech menstruation products like period underwear, so I relied on the products at the time (pads and tampons) that were often unreliable in my extreme circumstances.

I had been off the pill for about five months when I went to the doctor and explained what was happening. I wanted to ensure everything was working okay, especially given my age and cycles.

> **I never imagined my life without children.**

During this time, we bought all the gadgets you could get, from reading my temperature to determining my ovulation and the best time for sex. I love gadgets, and how many there are in the infertility world did not disappoint. I did acupuncture, drank different herbs, and tried all the latest fads. After all, you would try anything and everything to have a child. I thought we would get a plan and work through the plan, and we would become parents eventually. I never assumed otherwise—it is natural to be a mum, right? It's nature and something innate I felt I must do and would do easily, or so I thought.

Everyone around us seemed to be pregnant during this time, and this was hard, mainly because people still ask you questions about when you are starting a family or what's happening. Sex became mechanical and not as pleasurable as it was reduced to timing and actions before and after. This also led to some challenging times with undertaking multiple pregnancy tests and feeling excited, only to be disappointed again and again. My body was letting me down, and each negative test felt harder and harder, and we had not even started fertility treatments yet. They do not tell you it's normal for it to take time, as you often hear about those who seem to conceive by just looking at each other. Well, that's what you think!

My doctor started running tests…

Al was tested first as he was easier. He either had 'swimmers' or he did not. Yes, he had swimmers. His sperm was healthy and strong and had high mobility.

He was not the issue!

Then it was me, test after test. For me, it was several tests and being prodded and probed a lot. My tests at the time (as outlined earlier) concluded that I had PCOS and was not ovulating properly. This could be one reason we were having trouble. With this diagnosis of PCOS and my ovaries not functioning normally, we were going to need help to get pregnant.

I felt so lonely. I wondered why I was the only one.

Assisted Reproductive Technology (ART) Treatment

We needed help. I was infertile, and we needed to look at Assisted Reproductive Technology (ART) treatments. These types of treatments can vary from hormone medication (tablets and injections) to various procedures, such as Intrauterine Insemination (IUI) and In Vitro Fertilisations (IVF), using both donor or partner sperm and eggs, both frozen and fresh. There are numerous treatments available, but finding the right one is an individual process. I progressed to medication, and then we moved on to IVF.

And so began the cycle of disappointment and the fun and games of the IVF process, and doing all this while we both held down careers, studied and tried to get on with life as best we could.

In 2004, when we first started our journey, the resources for infertility were not as available as they are today. Any information about fertility, infertility, or the clinics and their success was around, but it wasn't easy to find and not in a way you could compare with now. There was nowhere you could easily go to understand what was happening to you or what your options were. We relied heavily on our doctors, the groups I was part of, and the information they provided. In researching for this book, I have seen more relevant information, access to financial and emotional support and services, and research that is now far more available to anyone and everyone.

In Australia, some of our costs are subsidised, but not all of them, and not for everyone, with some groups still missing out. Rebates are mainly paid when you have been referred for fertility treatments by your doctor, but this does not cover all costs and all tests. There are several variances depending on individual circumstances, including the reasons for treatment, the type of treatment and the clinic you attend. It is important to do your own research on this. This support was limited when we were undertaking our treatment, but thankfully, it is now more accessible for many people.

Today, there are also more support groups through social media and other channels that will help people feel less alone and provide them with additional support. There is also much more information on actual clinic success rates and how they compare, as historically, this information was not clear or widely available. But even with all this, the process still puts you in a cocoon and makes you feel alone.

While the focus from the WHO and the commitment they are making to address infertility and improve fertility care across the globe is still a work in progress, I am optimistic that it will lead to increased investments. This includes greater subsidies and better-funded research, enabling more individuals the opportunity to become parents, regardless of their circumstances.

The Statistics

When we were undergoing our fertility treatment, the breadth of statistics I see today was not as widely available. Today, the Australian Government and various organisations have invested heavily in providing the data necessary for individuals to understand their potential chances and help them prepare for the treatment process. An example of the shift in the availability of information today is a site called yourfertility.org.au, which has a large amount of data and information. It is a government-funded coalition of five specialised organisations that have united to provide information and facts about fertility for everyone, including the most up-to-date research. Unlike today, we did not have access to this type of information in one central place that was easy to find and navigate to guide us through before, during and after our journey. Seeing this now makes me glad that those going through similar experiences today have accessible, easy-to-understand information.

So, what does the data tell us about IVF success, and what were my actual chances of conceiving? I thought we would just do one cycle and bam, we would be pregnant!

According to research from the University of NSW, the range of IVF success is between 10-30%, depending on age, and most people are unsuccessful after their first cycle. This success rate diminishes as the person gets older.[32]

We did not have this information available when we went through IVF; we just thought we would be successful after the first cycle, as everyone else seemed to be, and the data available at the clinic was unclear. Thankfully, the research available now will help those going through this process understand what the realistic outcome of IVF may be for them. They will have information available that we did not have, including that you cannot expect to fall pregnant on the first attempt and that it may take up to three or more cycles to achieve a positive outcome. This is especially important given each cycle's significant financial and emotional toll. Having this information available when we started would have been extremely beneficial. It would have enabled us to make fully informed decisions and set realistic expectations, especially knowing we would need to fund multiple cycles and the subsequent financial burden and the setbacks it caused as a result.

When we began our 'cycle of disappointment' in Australia in 2004, there were 41,904[33] treatment cycles compared to 108,913[34] in 2022. Given the high volume of IVF procedures now undertaken annually, it is vital that we improve our knowledge of the causes of infertility and the ideal conditions to enable success. Understanding an individual's unique circumstances and chances can empower them to make informed decisions that maximise their chances of having a child. Some emerging information about factors like age may help guide individual choices in fertility decisions and treatments.

∼

It was not going to be just us making a baby.

Given infertility is a medical condition and fertility treatments are medical procedures, they come with various aspects that can impact your daily life, from disrupting your work to how you engage with friends and family. This was challenging when we were both trying to maintain a normal life, hold down our jobs, and manage our emotions. There were spontaneous challenges we couldn't always plan for, including medical appointments and navigating our feelings of heartache, anger, sadness, worry, guilt, hurt and envy.

One thing we discovered during this time was that making a baby involves more than just us. It was going to take a large village where all different people with different expertise were involved, providing overwhelming amounts of information and continuously prodding and probing me and my body.

During the process, you cannot help but think; what is wrong with me? What did I do to deserve this? It felt like it would never stop, and it would never end.

Why me?

Life throws many challenges at you, and infertility is certainly one of them. A huge one!

My Top 5 Evolutionary Insights

1. Relinquish control. You cannot control the outcome, but you can do everything to put yourself in the best possible position.
2. Educate yourself on the process and the potential outcomes.
3. Prepare for the end while staying positive and optimistic.
4. You are definitely not alone.
5. Talk about it! Find what will work for you and join an online group. Listening to others can help.

"I trust that everything happens for a reason, even when we're not wise enough to see it."
(Oprah Winfrey)

THREE

The Cycles Of Disappointment

The IVF Journey

"Grief is like the ocean, it comes on waves ebbing and flowing. Sometimes the water is calm, and sometimes it is overwhelming. All we can do is learn to swim."
(Vicki Harrison)

What I told myself
We will be parents.
We just need to navigate this process.
Everyone is successful.
Surely this will work. I just need to stay optimistic.
I only need one egg. Easy, right?
This feels so lonely. Why are we the only ones experiencing this?
Why does no one else have to go through this?
I feel sad and disappointed all the time.
I am sick of feeling sad all the time.
The cycle of disappointment is not an effective way to live.

I was infertile! Al and I needed help if we were going to have children.

Looking back, I was ten when the first IVF baby, Louise Brown, was born in 1978 in England.[35] This was followed by the first Australian IVF baby, Candice Thum, born in 1980, only the third in the world,[36] and only 24 years before we started our IVF journey. No wonder my generation never spoke about anything to do with people struggling to have children, and certainly not about infertility or IVF or any other treatments. In fact, we never knew much or spoke much about fertility. We understood little about what any of it really meant.

The world of IVF was growing, though, and by 2023, over 270,00 babies have been born through IVF across Australia and over 7 million globally.[37] In the year 2000, there were 5,466 assisted conception babies born in Australia that year.[38] In 2021, over 111,000 cycles started, with over 20,000 live births recorded.[39] This could either be an indication of the availability and improvement in ART treatments, the age of those giving birth or simply a reflection of the prevalence of infertility.

Over the past 40+ years, IVF technology and processes have come a long way and continue to help people with medical or circumstantial infertility to have a family. However, the technology is not yet able to make up for the decline in fertility that happens as women get older. According to yourfertility.org.au, the chances of falling pregnant after one IVF attempt is around 30% for a woman under 35, with a drop to 10% for women between 40-45, and then down to nearly 0% when over 45.[40] These are stark statistics, and yet we continue to fail to effectively educate young people about this.

While the IVF process has advanced considerably since the first IVF baby was born, and since I started my cycles of disappointment in 2004, with new approaches and methods for all stages of the process, it remains a process full of confusion, grief, loss, and financial burden. It still often takes multiple rounds to succeed, and several mental, emotional, and financial challenges come with that. The average cost of IVF in Australia can range from $8,000 - $10,000 per cycle,[41] depending on the individual and if there is funding support from the government and private health funds. According to Forbes Health, the average cost of IVF in the US is much more variable, depending on the clinic you go to and your needs. Still, on average, a single cycle could cost anywhere from $15,000 to $30,000 USD, with the medications alone accounting for up to 35% of the costs.[42]

Given the financial burden of IVF, some financial assistance is needed. While we have already seen various Australian legislation and codes of practice introduced to provide avenues to reduce this financial burden, they are still not universal. In the state of Victoria, where we underwent our journey, the legislation has been updated to further reduce the financial burden of fertility treatments on people seeking IVF, including the expansion of areas eligible for reimbursement to include reasonable costs associated with surrogacy. This legislation also helps regulate treatment procedures to promote safety and reliability, encourages and supports research around infertility, and provides for the safekeeping and provision of easily accessible data and information. This is a significant way forward in aligning with the WHO goals and its ambition of having children as a human right for all. While this is great for all with infertility today, the journey through IVF and trying to conceive had far greater limitations for us in 2004.

> ***IVF is a rollercoaster of pain, grief and small pockets of happiness that ultimately end in disappointment.***

So, let's be real here for a minute. IVF is a challenging process that is expensive, time-consuming, all-encompassing and a rollercoaster of pain, grief and small pockets of delight and happiness that can then progress to end in disappointment. It takes over your life and is not guaranteed. You need patience through every step, and sometimes you don't get beyond the first step. And every time you miss a menstruation cycle, you are wondering, *could I be pregnant?* There are big highs and many devastating lows. It is a process that disappoints you more than excites you.

It sucks!

When we started the IVF process, we believed it would just work as we mostly heard about the happy, successful stories and not much about those who didn't succeed. At the start of the process, we did not know much, nor did we have a guide to help us, and we assumed it would just happen straight away. Resources were not as readily available as they are today. Information about IVF was around, but it did not really tell you much about you or your issues and certainly did not tell you how you were going to feel during the process. Fast forward to today. There are more discussions and support groups to help you feel not so alone and give you information relevant to your circumstances.

Available Information

Resources I have looked at today are vast and have a lot of information, and some are well worth reviewing if you are in the middle of your journey. Fertility clinics are now offering more transparent data, along with researchers and universities publishing clinical facts and providing some of the most comprehensive reports on ART success and outcomes. These are easily accessible and shared more broadly than they were back in 2004, even if they existed back then. This type of information access and data transparency is critical for those going through the IVF journey.

One particular difficulty we faced was choosing a clinic that would be most appropriate for us without the availability of information that there is today. At least now, there are some guides on success rates and clinics that specialise in various issues, such as those that have more experience in treating older patients or more complex forms of infertility challenges. Clinics also vary their treatments, which varies the success statistics—some more successful and some less successful—so it is essential to do your homework when choosing a clinic. I don't recall any of this information being available in 2004, so we decided on our clinic without question based only on the doctor we were referred to and without a clue about the success rates. We didn't even consider this part of our process when choosing the clinic. Luckily, we found a good specialist straight away. One that we related to, so we went with the first specialist we saw.

While our specialist provided us with lots of information, success rates were never that clear to me throughout the process, and I did not dive deep into it. I trusted the process would just work. I think some of that comes from not wanting to know, assuming it did not matter, and not wanting to face the reality that it may not work, but also from not having additional independent data points to compare ours with.

In assessing the information available today, the success rates for IVF differ widely, depending on many different circumstances. It's so crucial that you look at the information yourself. Research as much as you can and tap into any resources that can provide you with information that can help you decide if IVF is right for you, including resources that provide independent data on clinics and success rates. However, I would use this information cautiously and in consultation with your specialist.

From our journey, I have learnt that everyone is different when it comes to infertility, so what works or does not work for one may or may not work for another. It's an individual thing, so I learnt quickly not to compare my journey to others. While we feel similar and go through similar grieving and pain, it will be different for each individual or couple.

The IVF Cycle of Disappointment

In addition to the statistics available, the other information that was critical for us to understand was the IVF treatment cycle and what it comprised. Our cycle consisted of six key steps, including:

1. Ovarian stimulation
2. Egg retrieval
3. Fertilisation
4. Embryo Culture
5. Fresh embryo transfer/embryo freezing
6. Pregnancy test

With PCOS, my egg quality and quantity were a challenge and this created issues for me throughout the IVF cycles. I did not respond well to the medication, and I did not get eggs. This meant that my chances of even getting to the embryo stage were extremely low.

While today, IVF technology and science have come a long way, there are still unexplained or hard-to-explain fertility responses like mine, where my ovaries didn't respond to the maximum stimulation and medication. However, the research I now see points to me being a Poor Ovarian Responder (POR). POR equates to 20% of patients going through ovarian stimulation for IVF.[43] The evidence around those with POR shows that they have disappointing outcomes using their own eggs, including lower birth rates and higher cancellation rates.[44]

This was me!

Now I know why it did not work!

Although IVF is a six-step process, our attempts never got beyond the first step, which involves hormone treatment to stimulate the ovaries to produce eggs. We needed many follicles to go beyond this cycle stage, so all my effort was to try to get more than one follicle with one good mature egg.

'It only takes one egg' was a catch cry we often used throughout this process.

Throughout the entire process, I did not get any stimulated follicles and, therefore, did not get the opportunity to retrieve any eggs during any of the cycles we attempted. Each cycle we started was cancelled, and each time we had to cancel a cycle, it was heartbreaking. This led to my medication being continuously increased until I was on the highest dose possible with continued poor responses.

It was grief, disappointment, sadness, anger, shock, and exhaustion.

My scans only ever revealed one tiny follicle, so all but one of my cycles were ultimately cancelled post-stimulation. Getting that one tiny miracle follicle enabled us to move to an IUI cycle, or 'turkey baster style' as it became known, due to the tool used.

The question we kept asking was—should we keep trying or should we stop? Our last attempt was when we switched mid-cycle to IUI and the turkey baster. We had some hope that the one and only follicle I got would release an egg at the time Al's sperm was put inside me, using the turkey baster. I remember the excitement we felt when I had one follicle. We had not had that through the entire process, so we thought, wow, this might just work. I remember we celebrated that one tiny win.

It was important for us to celebrate the wins, no matter how small.

But it did not work!

No one can be prepared to hear they are infertile or that they will not get pregnant, even after IVF. And while the whole reason for IVF is to get pregnant and have a baby, it's not guaranteed. Each test and cancellation brought us more grief. The process we went through was brutal. We got our hopes up every time, only to be disappointed again, which restarted the grieving process. Each cycle was emotionally devastating, and then it would need to begin again.

Along with the emotional rollercoaster, this journey included a vast number of challenging decisions and activities that we struggled with throughout, including:

- Research, research, and more research to find data and understand the complicated world of IVF and infertility. Research and data we could find were gathered and read to understand the complexity of not only my PCOS but also what options we had available and what this would mean.
- Tests, tests, tests, tests, and more tests. I don't think this ever stopped, and they were mostly reactive, so it was hard to plan my week, let alone my days around them. This included blood tests and more blood tests, whether for hormone levels or indications of how my body was functioning. I was like a pin cushion.
- Pregnancy test after pregnancy test. So many that I lost count.
- Many, many, many doctor appointments and consultations.

- A vast group of specialists, including doctors, nurses, radiologists, pharmacists, counsellors, eastern health practitioners, an acupuncturist, a nutritionist, a reiki practitioner, and the list goes on and on and on.
- Joining groups of women with similar issues and learning about my body and the impact of PCOS – and while little was known at the time, there were groups trying to understand it and how to minimise the impact of it on your fertility.
- Group counselling with others in similar situations.
- Scans, scans, scans, and more scans. Internal scans were especially hard, so much so that I named the tool (a long, thin ultrasound) used in the scan Roger (from the old cartoon called Roger Ramjet). I became very close and intimate with Roger. He was my bit on the side, and I saw him often during this process. He was not fun, and he was not pleasant, but he was necessary.
- Minor and major surgeries.
- Cubicle masturbation and sperm collection.
- Injections, injections, and more injections every morning and night, bruises and holes everywhere, especially around my belly and my arms. Hormone stimulation twice a day and at the highest dose, and yet still nothing. Al gave me every needle, so I did not have to do it myself.
- Even more hormone injections on top of the stimulation ones.
- All the various side effects, including bloating, headaches, nausea, mood swings and the emotional rollercoaster.
- Using the turkey baster method (IUI) to transfer sperm where it needs to go as you are about to ovulate.
- Carrying Al's sperm in a hurry across Melbourne in a paper bag to meet the time frame for the turkey baster.
- Money, money, money, money, and more money.

- Lack of decision-making about our future and what we would do next. We were at a standstill, frozen in time.
- I tried every diet, ate all the right things, and tried to get my body into the best shape it could be, but my body was fighting back, and my PCOS was not helping.
- Then there are all the legal decisions you must consider before you even start. If you have eggs left at the end, what do you do with them? How long do you hold onto them?
- For some, it may be the need to travel to other parts of the world to get the treatment needed at the time, which was challenging for many, especially during COVID.

The Devastating Impact of COVID-19

I cannot write a book at this time without mentioning COVID-19 (COVID) and the devastating impact that this had on people trying to be parents. Not only did some treatments stop, but many were also put on hold and even may have added to the burden and age impact that comes with trying to conceive. This process must have been devastating for those near the end of their journey or at an age that tipped them over the opportunity to try, resulting in many changing their plans during this time.

The Australian Institute of Family Studies research reports that during COVID, 1 in 5 Australian women under 40 changed their plans of having children, with 14% delaying the process and 5% indicating that they were likely to have fewer children.[45] Other findings in this report include that some were affected because of the delays in IVF treatment that were suspended during COVID. Many of the changes in plans are related to financial and job security concerns, along with the health risks associated with COVID or simply running out of time. In addition, Australia saw a record-low fertility rate in 2020, with 1.58 babies per 1000 women compared to 1.74 in 2018. According to the Australian Bureau of Statistics, this could have been attributed to COVID disruptions.[46] Yet despite all this, I also know of some successful people during this time using ART treatments, so that is something to celebrate as well.

The IVF process continues to evolve year after year, and as expected, today, there are some aspects of the process that were not around when we went through IVF. Most of them are positive, but some seem more invasive, particularly with the new requirement for those wishing to do IVF to have a police check, plus other requirements that are now mandatory. I appreciate that this is now mandatory. However, it still makes me angry that those who need to have kids through IVF are now required to have a police check, whilst no one is asked to have a police check before they naturally fall pregnant. I am still not sure I understand the need for this and what it is protecting when it is a human right to have a child, no matter what process is needed to achieve that, and those undertaking ART treatments do not do this lightly.

I learnt through this process that whilst it is challenging and hard, you will get through it and be okay even if unsuccessful.

It does get better!

> **Stopping is one of the hardest decisions to make.**

Al always said when you want to stop, we can stop. We did, but stopping was one of the hardest decisions we had to make throughout this entire process.

My Top 5 Evolutionary Insights

1. Get a good medical team behind you and ensure that you and your doctor work well together and have a strong connection.
2. Do your research and educate yourself so you are fully informed and can guide your outcome. Don't just rely on the clinic for guidance.
3. While reproductive science is incredible and has achieved some amazing results, it may not work for everyone. You need to be prepared and consider what this would mean if you were unsuccessful.
4. You should have a clear end in sight; otherwise, your life may only revolve around this when you have so much more to do, give, and achieve.
5. Be prepared for a rollercoaster of emotions, and allow yourself to grieve in your own way rather than how others expect you to. Make sure you celebrate the wins, no matter how small. You will need some excitement and happiness along the way.

"Flowers grow back even after the harshest of winters. You will too."
(Jennae Cecilia)

FOUR

Feeling Stuck Inside Our Cocoon

"We are all broken.
That's how the light gets in."
(Ernest Hemmingway)

What I told myself
It feels like we are stuck.
We cannot make any decisions.
Why does it feel like I have lost something
I never had in the first place?
Why am I so sad?
What is wrong with me?
This is not the right way to live.
We need to take our lives back.
I cannot make a decision.
Am I normal?

Our life was on hold, and we were in limbo.

It engulfed our lives completely.

The cycle of disappointment left us paralysed and unable to make decisions due to the uncertainty. We were completely stuck. We did not make any big life decisions because we did not know whether we needed to consider kids in those decisions. We both felt stuck in our roles and careers, and our important life decisions were put on hold while we waited to become pregnant.

We did not know who we would be or how to fit in without children. Many around us were parents or becoming parents. It was natural to want to be a parent. We were happy for them but extremely sad for us at the same time.

I was always in tears, and life revolved around this thing we could not get or have. It was so overwhelming it was hard to do anything other than work, sleep, eat and IVF. Al supported me throughout this process, and we supported each other.

We just had to get on with it.

> ***We had to ask ourselves if we were chasing something we may not even want now.***

Throughout this process of trying to have kids, it felt like sometimes we were just running on a treadmill that we could not get off. You also start to wonder if you are going through all this because you want a child or because of the challenge of it – we've started it now, so we must keep going until there is a positive outcome. You don't want to lose or not be in control. During the process, we often stopped and asked ourselves why we were doing this. We needed to confirm with each other that this was something we really wanted and not something we were persisting with to beat the process and win rather than for the reasons we originally began. We felt it was critical to do this with each other rather than get lost in the process. We had to ask ourselves if we were chasing something we may not even want now.

So, we chose to continue and persist with the the cycle of disappointment. While you are in it, the cycle of disappointment is a bubble. It felt like we were stuck in a cocoon where we were the only two in the world doing it. It was such a personal journey that it was hard for others to genuinely understand what we were going through if they had not experienced it themselves. Because no one talks about it, we felt so alone.

We felt like the only ones in the world who had been unsuccessful through the IVF process. Like you're the only ones who are failing. And you are the only woman in the world who cannot have kids. That's how I felt every day.

People only talk about their difficulty if you raise yours. No one talks about it if you don't. But when you raise your experience, others talk about theirs, and you realise that so many other people have had children through the process. We must talk about it more, given how many are struggling with infertility or seeking help through ART treatment. I want this to shift so those going through ART don't feel like they are the only ones, as we did.

Grief

I was underprepared for how emotional the process would end up being, the lack of control we would have, and the loss and grief we would feel. Loss and grief are experiences that will stay with us forever. These feelings will never go away completely, but they have subsided, and it has become easier. We just need to acknowledge that these feelings are there and not try to stop or fix them.

No one can experience our grief for us, and we cannot experience theirs. Everyone will grieve differently. Even Al and I did.

> **Don't assume what someone needs; just ask them!**

Grief is a natural response to loss. For us, it was the loss of not obtaining something we desired. Our grief would sometimes plateau and then would come back in ebbs and flows. We didn't think multiple avenues of advice would have been effective for us or helped us through this because the loss we were, and still are feeling, is our own unique loss that no one else can truly understand. While we occasionally received support from well-meaning and caring people, more often than not, they missed the mark and unintentionally created more sadness in us. This doesn't mean that people should stop trying to support those grieving, but perhaps look at the situation more closely and approach it with greater sensitivity and understanding rather than assume you know what they might need. ***You could just ask them!***

An important aspect of our grief was not to assume we needed a lesson or that we were bad or had done something wrong. Things just happen to people, and maybe there is no reason for it, or maybe there is, but at the time, hearing people tell us that everything happens for a reason did not help, nor was it something we wanted to hear. It made us question ourselves and any flaws we had that could have led to this situation. While I do believe everything that happens has a purpose to it, which has certainly been confirmed for us over the years, it was not something we needed to hear in the moment. What we needed was support during this time, and knowing that we had our family and friends around us when we needed them and that we were still important to them was enough.

We managed to grieve in a way that helped us both, but we were very different in how we dealt with the loss of being a parent. I have found that the journey of grieving is a journey that is unique to each individual and does not play out for anyone in the same way, even when you are grieving for the same thing. I learnt for myself that no one else could take away the pain and suffering I felt. I had to navigate my way through that and find ways to ease the suffering and sadness and fulfil other life goals and dreams. I needed to find what made me happy for me, as did Al. And we both had to discover what made us happy as a couple to get through the pain and stop the suffering.

"Pain is inevitable, yet suffering is optional."
(Buddha)

By the end of the process, we had lost all our hopes and dreams and all the things that come with having children and the lifestyle that brings. Grief is a natural response to this loss, and our feelings during this time were unpredictable. We did not go through a clear cycle of grief; we were just surviving.

I felt I had lost myself and who I was, and I still feel like I left a part of me back there.

There was also a feeling of shame for not being a real woman. I felt like I was a failure. I needed time to heal, and I needed to grieve in my own way.

Grief, for me, was not always sequential. There were times when I experienced exceptionally large ebbs and flows of happiness and sadness, which I would then get through, only to return to being angry and sad again. Grieving for the loss of future plans hasn't been so straightforward as aspects still come up now that I had not considered, and this causes additional grief. In my day-to-day life during the process, emotions varied widely. One day, I was happy, the next, I was extremely sad, and then I was angry. My emotions were heavily influenced by the outcome of the various tests or the doctor visits I had, both of which were regular. Having to deal with my grieving and out-of-control hormones was a pretty crappy time for us and those around us. Throughout this process, I felt like I had lost myself and who I was, and I still feel I left a part of me back there.

What was important to me during this time was not to bottle up my loss, and how I felt; when I did this, it made it worse. I needed to talk about it, get support, and confide in someone I felt comfortable with, though this was not always the same person. An important aspect of getting support from family and friends is to remember that they may also be dealing with their own challenges that affect their lives, causing pain, suffering and grief for them. Everyone has something that impacts them. I don't think I have ever met anyone who hasn't faced some challenge or experienced some form of grief in their life.

It's a challenging, hard and lonely journey. My grief was not clearly defined; it varied from month to month and from cycle to cycle. However, I can tell you that when I was first diagnosed with infertility, my feelings were very clear—I was in shock and a bit of denial about how and why this could happen to me. Then I went through a period of saying to myself, "This is fine; the science is on our side; we will be successful and have a child by the end: surely, I will be a mum." But as the process continued, anger took hold. Why us? Why no one else?

> ***Everyone has something that impacts them!***

I think the next phase for me was sadness and maybe depression, so we isolated ourselves from others, especially those who were pregnant or from significant events involving children. We did this when we felt like we could not face the grief we would feel associated with the event.

Finally—and I am definitely here now—is acceptance and ensuring I am leading a fulfilled and happy life, finding and pursuing things that give me joy. While there will continue to be other triggers that may set me back a few steps in the grieving process, I feel I have reached a place of acceptance.

I believe this journey of grief can also be true for anyone who already has a child but desires more yet struggles to have more children. While some people think, 'Well, you're lucky you're already a parent,' it doesn't lessen the feeling of loss they will still experience. Although their loss may be different, it is still a loss, and they will grieve for not being able to have the family they had wished for. It is never black and white, and all situations are unique. Your journey will be your own, as we all experience different paths, from the devastation of multiple miscarriages, lost embryos or no embryos to no eggs, and more.

For me, the grief I was feeling was from the loss of what I had longed and hoped for, the loss of experiences I would never have, the loss of hope, and the loss of my ability to define who I am or whom I had planned to become. Grief in IVF is genuinely about mourning what you and your partner don't have and won't have. This grief impacts not only those undergoing the process but also their family and friends, who want to see them succeed.

What was frustrating through this process was that, especially at the end, we just wanted to get back to life and feel normal again. This took time, and there was clearly no definitive time frame for the pain and suffering associated with loss and grief to end. Many experts will tell you there is no normal timetable for grieving. We just needed to be patient, allow it to unfold, and make sure we acknowledged our grief. This was hard as we expected it to end when we stopped our treatment, but it was not going to, and we needed to allow ourselves the time it would take to grieve the loss.

During our cycle of disappointment, it was important to grieve during each cycle fully and take ownership of my feelings and how I felt during this devastating process. Going through both the physical and emotional impacts of treatment at the same time was extremely challenging, and I needed to allow myself time and space to go through the normal stages of grief and acknowledge how each one impacted us. There were many times I felt isolated and misunderstood, but mostly, it was a lonely process, and people said the worst comments without realising they were hurting us or even realising they had hurt us. We created a cocoon of safety with just Al and I. And whilst this can make you feel lonely and like you are the only one in the world going through this, it actually brought us closer together.

While everyone's journey is different for various reasons, I have found that anyone undergoing the IVF process feels similar impacts. There have been similarities during all my discussions with others going through the same process, including the feeling of sadness and constant grief for a loss that is extremely hard to explain, which for me felt like it was harder to work through because it was hard to name that feeling or articulate it to others.

As well as the feeling of grief, sadness, and loss, I also felt:

- Guilt
- Anger
- Stress
- Confusion
- Loneliness
- Depression
- Worry
- Hurt
- Envy

I found it really important not to get trapped in negative thoughts, as this would send me into a spiral of negativity. I made sure I focused on ways to overcome these feelings. I also found it essential to take a step back and not be too unrealistic about myself if I was not coping with everything going on and I needed to stop, breathe, and have a break. I did.

Along with those negative thoughts, there were aspects of the process that were challenging, including:

- It is sterile.
- It can be mechanical.
- It is full of many disappointments.
- There were many sleepless nights.
- There was a lot of pain.
- It was very lonely. Feeling like there was no one to talk to or anyone who truly understood.
- There was a loss of dignity.
- Feeling overwhelmed by the never-ending process.
- It was like being in a cocoon and feeling isolated.
- Having mechanical sex.
- Feeling like everyone around us was pregnant and did it easily.
- Feeling guilty when I felt angry or upset that another person was pregnant, and I still was not.
- My hormones and emotions were all over the place. I was unpredictable.
- My tolerances were low, and certain events triggered me, such as births, kids' parties, and Christmas time. This was and still is, hard.
- I felt like my body had failed me, and I had failed Al.

To elaborate further on one area that I found really challenging was watching others around us getting pregnant easily. It seemed like everyone around us was conceiving easily and quickly, but as the statistics show us, this may not be the case. People don't discuss their journeys, so it feels like everyone else finds it easy, just not you. I was surprised when I started sharing my experience at how many people are or have undergone assisted conception.

I never thought that when we started the IVF process, we would not be successful. You read the information available and hear about the success, but you don't hear about the failures. No one talks about it not working; it's only how it worked. The books you read, the podcasts you listen to and the shows you watch are primarily about how to have success, not what to do when you are unsuccessful.

With cycle after cycle being cancelled due to a lack of follicles and eggs, I would see the doctor each time to get the results. I would try to be optimistic, but I ended up disappointed each time it did not work. I would reach a breaking point and feel done with the process, but then I would think, what if the next one worked? So, we would try again. To help us, we set an end date for when we would stop, which enabled us to plan life beyond the treatment and have things to look forward to. Our specialist encouraged an end date as well. I was grateful to have a strong relationship with our specialist, and she helped me wherever she could; it was easy to communicate with her and work through what needed to be done and when. Having this strong relationship was one of the most critical aspects during treatment.

Then, just before my 40th birthday, I finally had a follicle that was worth exploring further. It was not big enough to extract eggs from, but maybe an IUI and the turkey baster would work. They used a tool that resembled a turkey baster to implant sperm while I sat in a chair with my legs up in stirrups. We had to collect the sperm and race it across town in a paper bag within the hour to get it to the clinic in time for them to put it in the turkey baster and implant it into me. We laughed the whole way there, working out what we would tell the police if they picked us up. "Sorry, officer, we cannot stop important sperm in the brown paper bag." We laughed a lot throughout the process and tried to find humour in the devastation this process brings. We found that laughter was essential, especially during difficult times.

But – **fail, fail, fail!** While I had been optimistic, it did not work, and it was time to put a line in the sand and move on.

> **Our toughest decision during this entire process was to choose to stop.**

Deciding to Stop

Our most difficult decision through this entire process was the decision to stop. Life is all about making tough decisions and choices. We stopped pursuing something we may never get and moved forward with our lives. We needed to reflect on what we had sacrificed by solely concentrating on having a baby.

In your mind, you never imagine that IVF will not work for you. You hear all the success stories, never the unsuccessful ones. For me, given I never got an egg, I don't think I even made the statistics that get referred to as most of these start from the embryo transfer stage. I never reached that point in the process, even after multiple attempts over almost five years and countless cycles.

IVF was affecting all the decisions we were making, from where we would live to how we would spend our money to our career paths, and we had to move on from this. I was tired, I was sad, I was bloated, and I had gained an enormous amount of weight. I was 40 Kilos heavier than I am today; enough was enough, and I was over it. My body and mind were a mess at the end of the process. So, I threw a party not only for my 40th but also for the end of this never-ending cycle of disappointment. Whilst it was a stop to the process, I still thought for some time that I could fall pregnant naturally; I'm not sure how, but I still had hope even if we had ended the process of fertility treatments (maybe that's my optimism).

When we stopped, while we investigated alternatives, we didn't pursue any other options. We looked at adoption, but it felt even more challenging than the IVF experience we had just come off. We were overwhelmed by the process and just said no. My age also affected us. We looked at egg adoption, but that was just not for us. We wanted our child; if we couldn't, we needed to come to terms with that. We had had enough emotionally and financially and needed to get our life back. We were so hurt and emotionally drained that we could not even bear to start another process.

∼

I really wanted to be a mum. I was heartbroken.

Your life can lead you down many paths, so if you are only focused on one thing, this could limit your potential.

We started focusing on doing and experiencing things that made us happy, both individually and as a couple, and we embraced those rather than pretending to be happy. We discovered we could not force ourselves to be happy. We needed to find what gave us joy, what energised us, and what made us feel happy without really trying. These were the pursuits that would help us escape the suffering and get us back into life. While they may not be the same as being parents, they can still be very fulfilling.

I find it extremely helpful to channel my pain into creative pursuits like painting and photography. Back then, I focused on what I had in the moment: my family and friends, learning new things, leadership and career, binge-watching my favourite shows, socialising, socialising, and more socialising, painting and photography, travel, giving back to help others and community work. I made time for all the activities I was passionate about. If it made me smile when I thought about it, I would pursue it, which I still do. This book is one of those things I have wanted to do and felt passionate about doing for some time. If this helps one other person, then I will be happy.

During the process, I completed some studies, which helped me take my mind off IVF and onto something else. Learning energises me, so this was perfect for me to do. It gave me some good distractions to occupy my mind. I finished a Master of Business Administration at the start of the journey and started my Master of Commercial Law towards the end, which made me happy. I felt like I had achieved something, enabling me to focus on something else and reduce my suffering. It also helped me to feel like I was in control of something.

We also focused on ways to help ourselves and each other along the journey. This included going on weekends away, many weekends, and having fun adventures; we made sure we communicated with each other every day, and we made sure we told people what was going on as we needed the support. I also needed to be mindful not to rebound into something else. At one stage, I fully rebounded into my career and forgot about Al, who was also trying to figure it out. He raised this with me and brought me back. I am grateful we can communicate with each other when we need to.

I found it helpful to share my feelings and my journey to help others understand the issues and losses faced by those experiencing infertility. I realised that the more people understood our situation, the more supportive and understanding they were. The problem is that we do not talk about infertility, which is a big issue for us all. We might not feel so alone or vulnerable if we felt more comfortable talking about it.

I also want to highlight that I have noticed a shift over recent years, with the topic of infertility becoming less taboo, specifically regarding IVF. If you consider the 2018 WHO confirmation that infertility is a recognised disease, then this significantly contributes to normalising this challenging and often complicated disease. However, we still have some way to go.

So, let's continue talking about infertility and our journeys to help and support others through theirs. It is so important that if you are experiencing this, you feel comfortable opening up when and where you choose—so you cultivate a shared community around you and help shift the stigma.

I never imagined not having my own kids.

I have learnt to accept that bad stuff happens. It's a part of living; while we are not in control of what happens, we can control how we respond. So rather than hiding under the doona and wallowing in it all, we needed to find a way to let go of it. I had to forgive myself. While I know now it was not my fault, I really felt like it was at the time.

As our lives have moved on, we have come to terms with the loss and have tried, wherever possible, to create new meaning around not being parents and the life we have and will continue to live. We have learnt to just move with the grief when it comes, knowing that certain things still trigger us and that we will respond to them in different ways.

The grieving process for me took some time, but healing does happen, and everyone is different. There were good and bad days, weeks, months, and years. Even now, I grieve for aspects I will not experience or feel.

It is essential to understand that grief is normal and will subside over time as you readjust your life and its purpose to something different, maybe even something greater than you could have imagined. Your life can take many paths, which all may be worth pursuing, but if you are only focused on one thing, this could limit your potential.

Through all of this, I learnt that we were, and are, stronger than we gave ourselves credit for, not only individually but also as a couple.

It is also important to acknowledge that those who have been successful in the process know and understand how difficult it can be to experience multiple losses and grief before achieving success. Their success is incredible, and it should always be celebrated.

My Top 5 Evolutionary Insights

1. Get up and get out of your cocoon and find what energises you and gives you joy.
2. Talk to people you feel comfortable with and find someone to help you process what's happening to you. Seek professional help if you need it.
3. You have to laugh because if you don't, you will cry every day. Look for humour wherever you can and find things to laugh about.
4. Allow yourself to grieve whenever you need throughout the process.
5. Find ways to make decisions that help you feel like you are moving ahead with life.

"A day without laughter is a day wasted."
*(**Winnie the Pooh**)*

FIVE

You Are Not Alone

Family, Friends, and Pets

*"Anything is possible when you have
the right people there to support you."*
(Misty Copeland)

What I told myself
How can anyone possibly understand?
They will judge me.
They will think something is wrong with me.
They will feel sorry for me; I do not want their pity!
They will try to fix me even though I cannot be fixed and have tried everything!
Infertility is a life-changing experience.

I lost myself during this time and I needed to find myself again.

While this process feels incredibly lonely, you are clearly not alone, with **1 in 6 individuals globally** affected by infertility.[47]

As discussed previously, one of the significant challenges with infertility is that it feels so lonely, like you are the only person going through it. No one discusses it. But when you open up about infertility, you discover many others who are also struggling with the process or who have gone through it. I know when I talked about it, I found it really helped me. During this time, I also felt like it was all my fault and that Al could go and meet someone younger and have kids. When I felt this, Al would stop me and reassure me every time I raised these thoughts. It is critical to talk about how you feel and not assume others know what you are feeling. If I had not told Al how I was feeling, I would have continued to suffer those feelings in silence. This would have generated unnecessary stress and grief, which was not helpful. I lost myself during this time and needed to find myself again.

While much of what we experienced was very private and part of our personal journey, and we would go into our cocoon at times, we did share with family and close friends, but they had their own stuff going on. I found it essential to share my thoughts and feelings with more than just Al, as it helped me navigate what was happening. It is such a personal and often lonely journey, but realising that you are not alone can make it easier to cope as you understand it is not just you going through this. Of course, there were days when I did not want to talk about it and just wanted to feel safe in my cocoon with Al. It was also important to give myself time away from the discussion. It can be all-consuming, so you need those downtimes as well. During these times, we would try to do activities and pursuits that make us happy and bring us joy.

My support network has always been one of the most important aspects of my life. Speaking with someone who has experienced similar challenges was helpful because they understood my situation and offered empathy rather than sympathy. It is so important to find those networks and connections. Thankfully, there are so many ways to do this today, especially with social media and all the various groups. I feel this is one of the benefits social media has generated, but it was not as available when we went through the process.

I understand why you may not want to share what is happening, but it can be helpful for people to know why you might not be your usual self. While this is a personal journey that you need to navigate on your own, I found that discussing my experience helped me gain the support and understanding I needed at the time. Having supportive people around you is so important. Even if you don't realise the impact until you are past all the trauma, they can make a significant difference in helping you get through these tough times. However, not everyone will understand your journey, and that is okay as well.

You can feel wounded by how others respond during this time. It's important to recognise that people won't always respond how you would like, and you will need to learn how to manage your feelings when this happens, as most will never understand the impact of their words. Like other life challenges, not everyone will understand or know how to deal with them all, and given that the IVF process is full of grief, from my experience, not everyone knows how to handle this grief. It is crucial to listen to someone who is grieving through the process without judging or offering solutions, as, believe me, they have likely tried and researched everything available. I know from my experience that our friends and family care, but sometimes they might not know how to express it in the most empathetic way.

The cycle of disappointment is isolating, and fertility treatments take over your life with appointments, blood tests, scans, investigations, and endless waiting for results, waiting for follicles to develop, waiting for your womb to be at the right thickness and scan after scan after scan to see how many follicles you have developed. Then, if you get through that stage, there is the wait to find out how many eggs you have, how many have fertilised and how many embryos have developed. There is always a wait for these results, and this can be harrowing.

Your family and friends are the most important people who will support you through this journey. While they may not all understand, and some are likely to be pregnant or parents themselves, you need to look beyond this and get their help.

One thing I found helpful was having a support network, and where I could find them, a community of people facing similar challenges, which eased the feeling of being the only person with these issues. It was crucial to have people around me who understood what I was experiencing and how I felt.

We were fortunate. Our friends and family, who understood what we were going through, supported us the entire way. I know it was tough for them, not knowing how to respond, and some were facing their own challenges and losses. It was important that I talked to them and explained what was happening. Even if they did not fully understand, they stood by me throughout and recognised why we may not attend all functions and events.

It is important to recognise that it was also hard for our family and friends. I know throughout this process, they felt helpless and did not know how to help, but just knowing they were there was what supported me. You cannot expect others to always understand what you are going through, as you may not fully appreciate their struggles either. We needed to find a balance, as most people have something challenging happening in their lives that they could also be trying to navigate.

Sometimes, I just needed to pick up the phone and cry, and that really helped me. Friends and family were there. They didn't try to solve the problem; they were just there. No one could solve this except for the science, the doctors, the specialists and the health care team we were under. Even then, it remained unsolved in our case.

Naturally, people want to solve a problem. I am a problem solver, so I understand what this feels like, but sometimes we learn we cannot resolve all the problems people face, and all we need to do is be there when and if they need us. Sometimes, just having and knowing I had people to talk to if needed was enough, even if I did not always reach out.

Our Support

While writing this book, I asked some of my family and friends how they felt during this cycle of disappointment. Some of their responses are included in this chapter, and I hope this will help others and their family and friends to understand as well. Common themes emerged from each of them; they all felt ***helpless.***

And while they could not fully understand what we were going through, they tried their best to support us. Just knowing they were there made a difference, and if I needed their help, I knew I could rely on any of them.

My Parents
After my mum gave birth to my sister, she got pregnant again before having me but unfortunately had a miscarriage when she was ill. She has some understanding of what it is like to have lost a baby, and her memory was also one of not having the experience spoken about. In fact, I did not know about it until I was in my early 20s.

When talking to my mum and dad about our journey, their reflections included feeling helpless and the need to just be there for us. They felt it was unfair that it was so hard for us to have the children we really wanted.

They thought this would just happen for us - after all, we were doing IVF, and everyone was successful through IVF! They felt optimistic for us. Today, they know and understand that we still go through periods of unhappiness from being unable to have our own children. And while they have acknowledged that we both try to support all our nieces and nephews when we can, they know it is different from having our own.

During it all, they felt that we both needed support throughout the process, given the effort we were giving and the focus our life had at the time. For them, the worst part was waiting for my phone call at the end of each cycle, with poor results each time. Their memory is of the sound of devastation in my voice and the tears that followed when each time it did not work again. I know their wish for us was that they could just wave a magic wand and give us the baby we longed for.

I would ring Mum and just cry, and I know from her perspective that she felt utterly hopeless and not sure how to help. But they helped by just being there and listening to me when I needed them to.

My Sisters
My sisters felt bad for us for going through all we did and still not being parents. For them, it was hard as they had children of their own and had very hectic lives. I know from discussions with them that they felt sad about what we were going through, as they always thought we would make great parents. There were many difficult moments, both with their children and their children's children, that were extremely hard for us to

enjoy. They recognised our struggles and felt helpless, particularly when they saw others having children in unstable relationships. They thought it was unfair for us not to be successful. At one point, they considered offering to be egg donors or even be surrogates but ultimately decided against it because they didn't feel capable of doing this, and this was not something Al and I wanted to explore.

Just like my parents, they felt helpless and didn't know how to best support us on our journey or what they could say to make it better. There were times when they felt guilty that they had got kids without having to try too hard, and now they feel guilty for experiencing grandchildren, knowing this is something we will not experience either. Interestingly, they were particularly focused on Al as they noticed that the men in this process often seem to be forgotten, with the emphasis primarily on the females who undergo all the medical procedures. They especially felt this, given we had always been clear that Al was likely to be the stay-at-home parent, and now he had to reassess what his life would be like moving forward without kids.

The advice from my sisters to others is to talk to your siblings about what they are going through, even if you have your own kids. It does not matter; just let them know you are there if needed. While this is the advice they would give now, looking back at the time, they felt they did not know what to do to help, so they thought they had done nothing.

And while it was hard for my sisters to understand, I always knew they would be there when and if we needed them. They always had been and always would be.

I just needed to ask.

My Brother
My brother told me he felt guilty about being able to have children easily, while I had to endure all the stress of treatment without it even working. He felt he just needed to be supportive unconditionally without bringing his emotions or biases into the situation and to avoid judging or assuming how we were feeling.

He also felt helpless, that he could not help us, and he wanted to support us in any way we needed and not say the wrong thing inadvertently.

He had to find a way to support us.

I knew he would have been there for us if we needed him. And that's all that we needed.

My Friends
One of my lifelong friends told me she felt hopeless while I was going through this difficult time. She expressed that she did not know what to do or say to make it better, particularly since I had always been so supportive and helpful to her through difficult periods in her life. In our discussion, it's clear that many others felt this way. It was challenging for them to know how to offer support to us.

She especially wants to tell others not to be afraid of saying or doing the wrong thing because, like any grief, there is no perfect solution, especially in this situation. Although you cannot make it right, you can be there for those around you going through difficult times and be there for whatever they need and whenever they need it.

She recalls how important it was for me to have a focus outside of the process that I could control, which she saw as my career and studies. This is not to diminish what I could achieve regardless, but she saw that it gave me a space where I could push myself to achieve and gain some control back in my life.

Her main memory of this time was feeling utterly helpless and guilty because she could have a child, and she felt that, as much as she tried, she could never know what I was going through. Especially when I was someone who loved kids so much and was destined to have them, she felt that my coming to terms with that must have been extremely hard. On the back of this, though, I feel like her daughter is my own, and we have joked together about this, saying how her daughter is more like me than her in many ways. She has grown up with us as one of the girls.

My friends were there for me during a difficult time, readily available for a night out without questions. And even as they navigated their own losses, they offered companionship when I needed it most.

It was important that, as friends, we stayed close, even in times when I wanted to lock myself away. When I needed them, they were there. I was extremely lucky during this time, with no friendships lost due to a lack of understanding of our situation. I know this is something others have experienced, so I am very grateful for my circle of friends.

My Husband

But through all this, the main support we had was each other. I felt guilty throughout the process because I could not give Al what he had wanted; the life we had desired with each other was no longer possible, and we had to find a different life. One of the biggest challenges I had was to stop that feeling of guilt and know that Al was beside me no matter what, and having children was not what defined our relationship.

Communication was key for us. We had to communicate and support each other throughout each step. We may not have always got it right, but we always circled back and talked.

I feel blessed that we have become stronger and more aligned at the end of this process and have discovered ways to lead a fulfilling and happy life together. This process is brutal, and some may not stay together. We have, and we have become stronger and more resilient because of it.

Al and I worked together to ensure we were discussing the process and how we felt through all the steps.

This had been an emotional rollercoaster, but we survived.

Our Dogs

During the process, we rescued a beautiful Blue Heeler named Bubbles. She gave us so much joy and was the best thing we could have done. This helped us focus on something other than ourselves and was what, I think, kept Al grounded through the process. Unfortunately, she had several health issues that we managed over the years to ensure they did not impact her quality of life. While she is no longer here, she had a blessed life as a Heeler; she loved the couch and the bed and ruled the house. She was with us until she was 18 ½, which is a great inning for this dog breed, especially one with challenges. She had a great life with us.

Dogs make everything feel better. They make us laugh, cry, and focus our attention away from our own struggles. Dogs are part of our family. They give us unconditional love and attention.

While it took us a couple of years, we now have another Heeler, a Red named Bear, who is a crazy mad dog that makes us laugh and cry most days. He has his own challenges and was not very well as a puppy, which has led to complications and weird and hilarious habits as he gets older.

We are big believers that people and animals come to you for a reason, and these two crazy dogs needed owners like us to ensure they got the best of care and had the best life they could have.

Bear is still going strong and as crazy as ever.

Professional and External Help
It is essential to seek professional help if you need support in navigating your feelings during this time. If it would be beneficial for you, consider reaching out for some kind of professional help. While we participated in counselling during the process, and I attended some

group sessions, it was not for us. We leaned on each other, our family, and friends to get through it, along with some guidance from the professionals.

> **Listening to other people's stories can offer comfort and support you may not have realised you needed.**
> **Be open to it.**

Most people do not discuss their experiences and may seek comfort from online support instead. Listening to and sharing other people's journeys can be helpful, especially if you find it difficult to open up to those closest to you. Personally, I found that opening up about my feelings was beneficial in my journey, as it helped me realise that we were not alone. Once I opened up, others did as well. For me, this was and will continue to be incredibly healing.

Sharing your feelings can be comforting, even if it feels overwhelming at times. Hearing about other people's experiences and journeys can offer comfort and support you may not have realised you needed. Be open to it.

For me, being open and seeking support from those around me, including at work, was a crucial step for me to cope with the stress and emotional rollercoaster of my journey. This approach remains just as important today as it was for me during the process.

It is crucial to tell people what you need. They are not going to be able to guess. You need to guide them on how to support and help you. Most friends and family mean well and genuinely want to help, but sometimes, they may inadvertently trigger emotions in you. When this happens, remember they are just trying to help you. I have not seen this as intentional by anyone, but it can sometimes feel that way. Throughout this process, it is really important that you don't let this overwhelm you and be open with them if it does impact you. Tell them so they know and can understand your situation better.

For those supporting anyone going through this, it's important you consider the impact of your words. Be there for them, tell them you are there if needed, and don't try to solve the issue. If you are a parent yourself, don't try to share advice or try to understand as you won't be able to, and you may inadvertently say the wrong thing and may make it worse. Just be there for them.

I don't want to diminish the challenges everyone faces every day, especially parents. I am sure it can be hard and overwhelming. However, we all need to be mindful that we don't know what others might be experiencing in their lives that could be affecting them. If you know or suspect that a friend or family member is going through a difficult time, it can be helpful to park your own challenges, even if just for a short time. Keep in mind that when your day is tough, your kids are annoying, or your morning sickness is not great, those struggling with infertility would gladly trade places and would love to feel like you are. So, try to keep this perspective in mind during discussions and consider what others might be navigating through.

Having the support of others in recognising our loss enabled us to address our grief and share our sadness. It was crucial for me that our loss was acknowledged and not simply dismissed.

Our support network was just there and ready to help, so just be there.

If you are around someone who is navigating challenges, please don't ignore it, avoid them, or even stop spending time with them. Acknowledge the pain they are feeling. It's important that the loss or grief they are feeling is acknowledged to ensure you do not make them feel even more isolated. If you know anyone going through this kind of loss, just making small gestures to acknowledge their pain may make a difference for them. I know it helped me. We did not need sympathy; having friends and family there for us and recognising how crappy the process was, was enough for us.

> **Most people are dealing with challenging situations in their lives that they may also be trying to process.**

What I recall has benefited me, and some ideas that may help others, in addition to just being there, could include:

- Asking if they want to talk about it.
- Asking what they need from you and never offer advice unless they ask for it or unless you have been through the same process and understand.
- Not minimising the experience they are going through.
- Do not offer solutions or share what you have read somewhere, as they would have researched it all and have read it all, trust me! They have undoubtedly heard about all the 'miracle babies' and 'miracle treatments.'
- Just focus on some of the things you should say rather than what you do say.

- Checking in on how they are, not just the results, and offering to help them. Hug them, be with them.
- Just letting them know you are there, and sometimes a distraction is the best thing for them, like a night out with the girls or a trip away. This always helped me.
- Not isolating them; still invite them to your events, especially around kids. They will decide if they want to attend and just be understanding if they don't come.

Just check in on them and ask simple questions like:

- How are you today?
- Are you doing OK?
- How are you feeling today?
- What can I help with?
- What can I do to help?
- What do you need?

If you are a friend or family member of someone experiencing this, ask them what they need from you. Let them know you are there and ready to listen. Try to understand what they are going through. Also, remember that they may not feel comfortable asking for help due to the overwhelming nature of what they are going through. You may need to reach out first.

Getting support and help from your friends and family or others going through similar challenges can be extremely beneficial. Friends and family provided us with great support and continue to do so. It is important to remember that those who love us don't always know what to say or do. Any offers of help, always came from a place of love and support. Just knowing they were there if we needed them was valuable and all I needed at the time.

And some days, we needed to park our issues and grief to help them through theirs. This was just as important.

My Top 5 Evolutionary Insights

1. You should talk about what you are going through and share it with family, friends, and colleagues.
2. Most friends and family have good intentions; they are just trying to help.
3. Talk about what you are experiencing to build a support network.
4. Friends and family are your rocks, but you need to be open and honest with them and tell them what you need and don't need so they know.
5. Be mindful of what your family and friends might be going through themselves. Check-in with them as well.

"Many people will walk in and out of your life, but only true friends will leave footprints in your heart."
(Eleanor Roosevelt)

SIX

Don't Forget Your Lippy

The Emotional Rollercoaster

"Pour yourself a drink, put on some lipstick, and pull yourself together."
(Elizabeth Taylor)

What I told myself
I have to get up today, don't I?
I feel empty.
I feel like a failure.
What if I just lie here for a bit longer?
No one will know. People won't see my sadness.
I cannot let others see how sad I am, can I?

I was close to my nan; she was an amazing woman. Amazing Grace is what she was known as. Growing up, she shared her wisdom and always encouraged me to put on a brave face and face the world, even when I felt I couldn't. She would tell me as I walked out the door, '**Don't forget your lippy.**' It was her way of saying that as long as you have your lipstick on, everything will be OK, and you can face any challenge. This stuck with me, and I continue to ask myself as I walk out the door: Do I have my lippy on? Am I grateful for what I have? And do I have a smile on my face, and am I getting on with it?

During this time, I felt all the emotions, sometimes for short periods and sometimes for prolonged periods. I could go from anticipation and elation to disappointment, heartache and despair all in one day and sometimes within one hour. It feels like a rollercoaster, and it's hard, but it's okay not to be OK through this process. The difficulty faced by those going through this is vast, so the navigation needed to be done by those around you is complex and confusing.

There are many support systems out there, including forums, blogs, community groups, and social media groups, that may help. There is often strength in seeing and talking to someone to help you get ahead of the issue, deal with the situation, and talk through how you are feeling and what's next. Despite all these support systems, it was still hard to stay above water, maintain a focus on my career and keep an outward happy face. It was crucial for me to put my lippy on and face the world when all I wanted to do was hide under the doona and make it all disappear. But we could not just live under our doona. We had to get up and get out because it's easy to fall into the trap of living in your cocoon during this time. We did for parts of this at times, but it was not helpful for either of us.

We learnt that grief is vital to deal with throughout the process and beyond. It does not just stop one day, and you are all good. All grief is complex and individual. Ours was and still is today. It's painful and does not go away. Occurrences happen day to day that are a big reminder. So, we needed to find coping skills and tools to help us when things hit without warning. Our grieving was for something we had never had and the idea of something we desired, versus the grieving from the loss of a person or a child. We did not suffer from multiple miscarriages throughout the process, so our loss was a loss of the idea of something we desired. For us, we were grieving for future losses that are difficult to really identify and understand fully.

Infertility for us comprised several negative aspects, including the financial, emotional, and social strain. The cost of each failed cycle and all the areas of life we put on hold were emotionally draining in many parts of our lives. There was also the social strain with all the babies and child-centred activities around us daily, stories and pictures on social media, family chat in the workplace, and with our family and friends. All of this increased my stress, anxiety, and sadness. Dealing with the stress and disappointment of infertility has recently been shown to be similar to the stress experienced by those with other serious illnesses,[48] so it's critical we understand this more.

The Things People Say

People will say and do things that hurt you during this time, but remember, they cannot understand what or how it will affect you. While you are in the middle of the grief and stress of this process, people around you will offer advice. It will seem like they think they are an expert telling you how to solve the issue. Remember, their intentions will always be for the right reasons. I know through my journey that everyone meant well, and no one went out of their way to make me feel bad or do or say anything maliciously, but in the process of heightened emotions, you can take innocent comments the wrong way.

I needed to stop and think before reacting to anything anyone said.

I used to say to myself:

- What is going on in their life at the moment?
- Do they realise what they have said?
- How can I give them feedback on what they said calmly and unemotionally?
- How can I help them to understand from my perspective?

Since then, I have heard many comments over the years about infertility that have always stuck with me, including:

- It's all the woman's fault. She did something to cause the problems.
- The woman focused on her career, waited too long, and is now infertile.
- Only heterosexual couples have issues.
- If the male cannot get his wife pregnant, he is not a man.

- You are not a woman if you don't have a child.
- If you cannot have kids, it's not like other losses, and you should just get over it and move on.

Often, you are asked after you get married, "Are you pregnant yet?". This question is always a hard one to answer and one that I don't think people should ask so directly. There were a couple of ways I dealt with this situation. Sometimes, I would laugh it off and change the subject, depending on who was asking. Other times, I would share that we are trying but having challenges and going through IVF. Most people, myself included, assumed that IVF would just work and that you would be a mum soon, especially back then. However, as I became more educated through the process, I tried to help others understand the reality of it.

How people reacted and responded to our challenges influenced how much we chose to share, depending on the reactions and responses we got. If you constantly receive negative responses and reactions, it discourages you from sharing your experiences due to fear of these hurtful comments. If you are around someone going through this type of grief, or you suspect it, then you should consider your words before speaking. Never assume they have made a choice unless they tell you directly. Additionally, be mindful of the questions you ask; you may not be aware of what they are experiencing in their lives.

Be mindful and think about what you are saying before you say it.

Over this period and beyond, many comments people make can trigger your emotions, so it is crucial you find a way to cope with this. In my mind, I called this the 'BS Lotto.' Whenever we heard things that impacted us or did not make sense, we would think, 'Here we go again.' This helped me regain control over my feelings and back from others. Most people don't even realise the impact of their words. People often say thoughtless, hurtful things, so it was important for us to detach from the pain and regain control. To manage my emotions, whenever I heard a few of these, I would buy myself something nice or have a massage or something similar to ease the pain. Comments can be hurtful, regardless of the reason why someone does not have kids, whether due to medical, circumstantial or personal choice.

Below are some examples of the conversations we have had and some that others have shared.

Why don't you just adopt?
Chances were slim for someone of my age when we stopped IVF, and then you needed time to grieve, so jumping straight into that process was not possible. We needed to wait six months post IVF. The process for adoption, at the time we looked at it, seemed to be just another emotional rollercoaster, so we decided that if we could not have our own biological kids, we would not have kids.

Maybe you gave up too soon?
Sometimes, this comes from those who fell pregnant easily and do not understand the cost emotionally, financially, and physically. Many people who are not parents are devastated, and they attempted for as long as they could. Telling them that they should have tried harder on the back of this devastating process will not help them at all. We tried everything we could.

It was just not going to work for us. Those who are going through this have tried everything possible, and people around them need to understand this and let it go as well. I imagine this can be hard for parents if they want to be grandparents, and you were their only hope.

But I read that...
Miracle baby stories are everywhere, and everyone shares them. They don't always work and can give false hope. Everyone is different, so what worked for one person may not work for another. They are called miracles because that is what they are. They are rare, and telling someone what you heard in the middle of this may not help them.

You are lucky to not have kids. You can do what you want when you want...
While this may appear true, this is not really the case and does not help. Whilst it provides us with other comforts, we would trade these to be parents any day, but that's not what our life is about now. We have to continue to find comfort in other things ourselves. We don't need to be told by a parent what this is for us or what it means for us. Our life is on a different path from the one we envisaged.

Have one of mine!
While I get why people say this – it does not help at all. In fact, it gets me mad. I want every parent to enjoy what they have and not take it for granted.

At least you lost the baby before you knew it or were too far along.
I had no words for this one when I heard that this was actually said to a couple who lost a baby.

It's so hard living with a pregnant woman - said to a man who had a wife who was trying to get pregnant.
Think about how this might sound and what this man might be struggling with, not only his emotions but that of his wife's, after many attempts and many hormone injections.

You don't know what you are missing out on, so what's the problem?
While this may seem like a logical point, we know what we had imagined life would be like as a parent, and this is what we are grieving. To say we do not know is insensitive and easy to say when you have it. We had visions, we had dreams, and they were real.

It will happen when you stop, like it did to X and X.
This is one I hear a lot and one that is not something you need to be subjected to when you are stopping this process. It is hard enough emotionally when you get to the end, so hearing there may still be a chance and having false hope creates a longer grieving time.

Relax, it will happen.
If only it was this easy, then we would not have this problem!

The above are a few things that we, and others, have heard over the years. For those around people experiencing this, be mindful and think about what you are saying before you say it. If it begins with, or sounds like you are, giving advice or suggesting they should look on the bright side, then perhaps don't say it. We received plenty of comments, such as, "Did you hear that...", "Maybe you should...," "Have you tried...," "I read the other day...," or "At least..." and the list goes on and on.

I believe part of this is due to most people not being very comfortable with grief and do not always know how to respond. From my experience, it seems that people, myself included, struggle to deal with grief when someone else is grieving. You might worry about saying the wrong thing, which leads to fumbling over your words and inadvertently saying something hurtful. Or worse, you say nothing at all, failing to acknowledge the person or their grief. Beyond my personal experience with grief, I now know how important it is to think before you speak and make an effort to acknowledge what the person is feeling. You don't need to solve the issue; you just need to be there.

The other challenge throughout this process is regarding sympathy versus empathy. I never wanted any sympathy; the last thing I wanted was for people to feel sorry for me. It is important to be open and discuss it. Do not feel sorry for us, as it can make us feel worse.

After reviewing various dictionary definitions of sympathy and empathy, I found that there are clear differences between the two. Sympathy involves having pity for someone and is an emotion experienced in reaction to something happening to someone else. You feel sorry for them. Empathy is about putting yourself in someone else's shoes and understanding what it feels like as you identify with them. You don't just feel bad for them; you align with their emotions and feelings.

> **Being a mum is something innate in you, it's not something you can just switch off.**

The Loss We Felt

We found it essential, as we navigated the cycle of disappointment and the opportunity to be parents continued to slip away, to prepare ourselves for what might be. We contemplated what life might look like without kids. I spoke to others who were child-free, and we discussed it as a couple. One of the biggest challenges we faced was coming to terms with the end of our journey to conceive and processing all our emotions surrounding it, including the realisation that we would be treated differently. Our finances and our emotional well-being took a hit, and we had to refocus on what our lives would become.

For me, it was important to identify, acknowledge, and address the emotions I was feeling both during and at the end of the process and to continue doing this. This included feelings of failure and guilt for being the cause of our situation. I also felt envious of others who seemed to achieve everything effortlessly (I know this is not always the case). I had lost my self-esteem and felt worthless, believing I was not a whole woman because I could not do the one thing that nature intended. Being a parent is something innate and it is not something you can just switch off.

We grieved for the loss of the experiences we would never have that you see every day around you, in the workplace, on TV, on social media and all around. This is the hardest part, and it is vital you allow yourself time to grieve for these losses, but you also need to move forward with your life and focus on working through how you will now live it.

While we lost nothing tangible, there is an enormous loss and grief associated with what we never got to experience and never will, including the loss of:

- Not having kids, creating our own family, and not having the family name continue.
- Never feeling what it's like to carry our child in my belly.
- Never seeing the 2 pink lines on a test (although COVID has changed that).
- Never hearing the heartbeat of another human that Al and I had created together; that was a mixture of both of us.
- Never experiencing morning sickness (I would have loved to have been unwell due to a child growing inside me).
- Never experiencing the pain of birth or the elation of holding your child for the first time.
- Never understanding what it is like to breastfeed.
- Never experiencing the excitement of Christmas morning.
- Never experiencing the first day of school, the last day of school, graduating from university, or getting their first job.
- Not holding a tiny hand in yours.
- Not throwing a kid's party.
- Not being able to comfort your upset child.
- Not seeing them grow up, get married, have their own kids.
- Not being able to give our parents grandchildren.
- Not having someone to take care of us unconditionally when we age.

- Not having someone to want our stuff or grieve for us when we die.
- Not having someone to show and help navigate everyday life with.
- Never being a grandmother or grandfather.

The list goes on and on. This is not about having anyone feel sorry for us but is about acknowledging and understanding those elements we grieve for and allowing ourselves to grieve for them. While we have some of this around us, with a hoard of nieces and nephews and now grand nieces and nephews, they are just not our own, so there is a difference.

I felt like I was not a whole woman.

Managing Baby Showers and Other Triggers

Trigger events for me during this period and, even today in some circumstances, were other pregnancy announcements, baby showers, Christmas, and holidays.

It is normal during this time to feel emotional regarding pregnancy announcements and baby showers, and it is okay for you to feel sad. I certainly did, and it's OK if you don't feel like attending - just embrace how you are feeling at the time and go with that. I tried to do most things as it was important to celebrate for the children and family and friends. It's not their fault I could not have kids. You need to remember that. But also acknowledge your emotions and how you feel. Friends tended to tell us individually rather than in large groups. This was helpful.

And it's okay not to go to events or engage, especially when you are in the middle of the process. Your friends will understand and should support you. There were many occasions where I just took myself out of the situation. When the time is right, you will be excited for friends, family, and colleagues who are having children, as well as those who are parents.

If you are the one celebrating, we are excited and happy for you and don't want to be treated differently, but we may need space and time to process, so make sure you give anyone going through this the time to come to terms with it. Tell them about the celebration directly, and don't be upset if they cannot attend all the events you want them to. Please be mindful of this and don't judge them. Don't ask for an explanation; support them. Don't feel like you cannot be excited yourself; just be mindful that it will be hard for those who are in the middle of this process.

Keep inviting them.

Social media can be an issue for those going through this process or those at the end. There are always posts celebrating babies or children, which should be celebrated, but at times, this can feel overwhelming. Don't feel angry if you don't get a 'like' from all of us; we may be triggered by what you have posted, so we may prefer not to look at it or read it.

I realised I could not be bitter about what was happening to me. I needed to focus on the aspects of our lives that were amazing and celebrate them. I focused on various ways to cope, including trying to stay positive and not be bitter.

I took a step back and acknowledged the wonderful things we had in our life, embraced those, got out from under the doona and applied various coping skills to manage it all. I still use these strategies today when I sense something might trigger my emotions.

∼

I can tell you that life doesn't always result in perfect planning and outcomes. It is a winding road that takes you in many directions, never in a straight line from one destination to another. I know our life is and will continue to be great, and I want to live it the best we can. Setbacks will always be there, and even if we had been successful through fertility treatment, there may have been something else that could have impacted our happiness and fulfilment - this is the reality of life.

If you are around people coming to terms with not being parents, either through medical or circumstantial situations, it is vital that you also accept the outcome for them. Just support and acknowledge it. Trust me, they would have tried everything possible and now just need to move forward with their life. From my experience, people in these circumstances need to create the most fulfilling life they can, which feels and looks different from what they had dreamed or imagined. We did.

You cannot stay hidden under your doona forever. You need to get up, get out and start living and enjoying all you have rather than dwell on what you don't have. For us, we had to grieve mindfully, and I had to let go of the guilt and create a positive mindset. We needed to build a better future for both of us.

Life is not always about perfect planning and outcomes. It is a winding road that leads you in many directions and never in a straight line from one destination to another.

Please remember, if you are going through something similar, your journey will be very different from mine. You cannot compare your journey to anyone else's because we are all unique, each with our own backgrounds, genetics, life circumstances, and experiences. How each person deals with and manages their situation will vary, but you should know that you are not alone.

Oh, and **'don't forget your lippy.'**

My Top 5 Evolutionary Insights

1. Avoid comparing yourself or your journey to others. Everyone is different.
2. Stay optimistic, and don't forget to put your lippy on as you walk out the door. This helps both you and others believe what is possible.
3. Don't take what others say personally. They just do not understand.
4. Get up, get out, and enjoy all the wonderful things life has to offer.
5. Get professional help if and when you need it.

"If you're sad, add more lipstick and attack."
(Coco Chanel)

SEVEN

We Bought A Boat!

Finding The Balance

"If your heart is broken, make art with the pieces."
(Shane Koyczan)

What I told myself
How could I possibly continue if I cannot be a mum?
That's what I wanted.
I feel better when we buy stuff.
I will focus on my career now and push through the pain that way.
This will solve all our problems and make the pain disappear. Won't it?
I need to find something that gives me joy.

I was forty, my body was a mess from all the drugs, my emotions were out of control, and Al and I were looking at each other, trying to work out what was next.

We needed to find ourselves again.

At the end of our journey, **we bought a boat!** We did. We were driving through a country town, saw a boat shop, stopped, and bought a boat. It had all the gadgets and even a custom-made cover. This made us feel great and free (cost aside). The boat was delivered, and then it spent the next 12 months in our backyard because neither of us got around to getting our boat license. I even bought Al a magnetic fishing game so he could sit in the backyard on the boat with a beer and pretend he was in the water. I wanted to call it *Aqua Phobic,* given it had not seen water.

We ended up selling the boat!

Maybe we were just not ready to move too far forward, and the boat represented that.

Although it was hard, we got some relief from spending money, buying new cars, and going on great luxurious holidays, much to the annoyance of our financial planner. *Sorry!* This was a part of our healing process, and we needed to do it to get through. Our way of coping was to buy stuff emotionally. I think Al would say I still do this today, and many an op shop or family member has benefited from my habits.

It was not my fault.

You have to accept that you will do some impulsive things at the end of this journey to fill a hole you cannot ever fill, and while some may not buy a boat—maybe it's something smaller or something bigger—it can work short term. What it did for us was make us feel better for a while, but long term, we still needed to deal with the grief of coming to the end of our journey to parenthood. And for me, at the end of this process, it was, and still is, hard not to feel guilty, especially when it was my body that I thought had failed us. I needed to stop feeling guilty about this situation. It was **NOT MY FAULT**, and I had to learn to love my body again.

But this can be hard to do, especially when it is you and your body with fertility issues. I had to find strategies to help shift the voice in my head that was telling me this. Life has so much to offer, and the last thing I wanted was to spend my life feeling guilty, chasing something we may never get, and wasting precious time.

You will never get that time back.

I needed to think positively, reflect on what Al and I had, and be okay with that. We had to reframe what happened to us and shape it into something meaningful and of value. And this book is part of that. How do I share and communicate what we have learnt from our experience to help others? It has been important to shape what I have gained from the experience into something that can benefit not only myself but also others in the future. We had to find other ways to define ourselves, move away from feeling stuck and take ownership of our situation. While we cannot control the world around us or our circumstances, we can choose how we respond to the challenges we face in our lives.

> **We have control over how we choose to face challenges in our lives and how we respond to them.**

I have chosen to embrace the experience, discuss it, and try to understand it rather than avoid it, hide it, or ignore how it made me feel. This allows me to create my own narrative around it, and I can now face the world head-on and choose what lessons I take from the experience, not only to help me but also to help others through similar journeys.

I have come to understand that it was my choice to be happy. Nothing was going to make me happy, so I had to focus on what brings me joy in the moment. I stopped comparing myself to others, and Al and I defined our own criteria for what success looked like to us. Even today, we celebrate our achievements, acknowledge our struggles, and respond in our own way rather than conforming to how others expect us to. We had to find our way out together, but also, we had to let ourselves grieve in our own individual ways.

I learnt along the way that it is normal to feel sad and disappointed when life does not go as planned and that we cannot always be happy. We need to allow time to grieve for any loss, but it's also essential to make sure we reflect on and learn from that loss, sadness or disappointment.

If your inner voice is negative, challenge that perspective. Instead, counter the negative with positive self-talk. Strive to find the positive in a crappy situation and shift the dialogue in your head. We had to change our focus to areas that brought us joy and made us happy. I had to practice having a nurturing voice in my head to make sure I was kind to myself. This included mindfulness and repeated positive affirmations. I prioritised ensuring that my inner voice was supportive and nurturing rather than critical or guilt-inducing.

> **Communication is the key.**

I redirected my energy towards other aspects of my life, including my career, which had been on hold. Initially, I had replaced not having kids with one thing—work and career—therefore, I failed to take the time needed to heal and find the right balance in my life. I was incredibly grateful when Al raised this with me, as it helped me refocus on the things that mattered rather than just my job. It was the best thing he did. I hadn't realised I was doing it and needed to be challenged. I am a 'jump in all or nothing' person and am grateful I had Al to guide me in the right direction to achieve the right balance. I had forgotten to give myself time to heal. It's essential to reflect on what you have redirected your focus to and try to rebalance your life as soon as you or someone else notices it. I am still not great at this today, but I try, and Al continues to raise it when he sees it, for which I continue to be grateful. As a partnership navigating this journey, we needed to communicate with each other regularly and not just make assumptions.

While you focus on getting on with living again, it's imperative that you stop and reflect rather than go full steam ahead as I did. I jumped in headfirst and missed everything else around me. You need to be mindful of this. During this time of disappointment and grieving, open communication with your partner, family, and friends is the key. Other stuff will happen, and you won't just have one challenge in your life. You may face many challenges that shift and change your focus and your plans throughout life. Learning how to manage and deal with this is crucial for your happiness and fulfilment.

I found that when we were forced to confront the reality of our situation, we discovered we were stronger, both individually and as a couple, which was rewarding. We focused on finding the things that brought us joy and helped change our thought patterns. Our resilience as partners going through our infertility journey and coming out stronger on the other side has set us up for any other challenges that come our way. We are stronger as a couple because we built this strength and resilience through the process.

I needed to find what energised me and brought me back.

Throughout this journey, I discovered what I needed to do to help rebalance my life. Some of the things I did include:

- Embracing my situation and accepting the reality of it.
- Being patient and accepting the outcome and what it meant for us.
- Allowing myself to be vulnerable.

- Embracing help and support in whatever shape that took.
- Keeping my brain and body active so I could keep moving forward.
- Not dwelling on what I did not have.
- Making sure I took time out (doona days) when needed.
- Saying no to stuff if it made me feel uneasy or sad.

I did many things during this time to help me get through. I focused on various aspects of both my body and my mind. Some worked for me, and some did not. Here are some of the ones I tried:

- Acupuncture
- Journalling
- Meditation
- Herbs
- Hypnotism
- Therapy
- Talking about it
- Reiki
- Massage
- Spending money and buying stuff that gave me joy
- Painting
- Photography
- Travel

What I found the most helpful was Reiki. It enabled me to find balance and helped me find areas I needed to focus on. Finding someone to support me during this time was essential, and Al suggested someone I should see who would help guide me in rediscovering those aspects of life that brought me joy. I am still grateful for that support, as it led me to reconnect with my creative side, which I had been missing for some time. I started painting and took up photography, both of which helped me achieve more balance and aided in my healing process.

I found it interesting how we shifted throughout our journey as we progressed beyond the grief and pain. When I began my painting, I was rush, rush, rush until the instructor advised me to stop, take it slow, and enjoy the experience. I owe her a lot. Not only did she help me create fantastic art, but she was also like therapy at the exact time I needed it. She helped me rediscover my creative side and taught me to slow down and appreciate the moment.

While all these activities make you feel better, in the end, it was connecting with friends and family and getting back into the real world that helped me the most. We got out and started travelling and living again. I spent regular quality time with friends and family doing weekends away and girls' nights out, and I cherish those times we had and still have today.

I choose to be happy!

It is really important that through these times, you identify the areas that can help you overcome the sadness and rediscover happiness. Some things we found helpful included:

- Mental stimulation through learning and developing myself.
- Celebrating any success, no matter how small.
- Nourishing our relationships, both personal and professional.
- Choosing how we responded to disappointment.
- Being optimistic in all situations. It's definitely something Al has helped me with.

- Having time for ourselves.
- Travelling in style.
- Having what we need or want when it suits us.
- Refusing to let things get us down or stop us from moving forward.
- Appreciating ourselves more.
- Being kind to ourselves and not beating ourselves up if things don't go our way.
- Moving on quickly from setbacks and disappointments.
- Having our animals around us with their unconditional love.
- Helping and supporting others.

Throughout all of this, it is essential that you are kind to yourself and not beat yourself up. This is, and can be, incredibly challenging, so I cannot pretend it is easy, but it's important.

This journey is an emotional rollercoaster, so you need to focus on the positives to help get you through. There is an enormous sense of feeling like you are missing out, but it is important that you accept the life you have and stop yearning for a life you will never have. I have learnt that while you cannot control the challenge, you can control how you respond. You can choose to let the things that challenge you control you, or you can choose to focus on the positives in what you already have in life. Infertility does not define us, and life will always bring challenges. What matters most is how we respond to these difficulties. Being infertile continues to affect me, but I choose to focus on the good I have, and I choose to be happy.

I can be grateful for what I have, and all I have accomplished, and for everyone in my life, all the people around me and those I spend time with.

We are fortunate to have children around us, and many will come and go throughout our lives. While they will not be our kids, they still play a significant part in our lives, and we hope they will continue to be around us for a long time yet.

The choices we make are up to us and us alone. I choose to live an optimistic, happy, and fulfilled life, even if it is different from what I imagined for myself and us. I have chosen to embrace this part of our life.

I choose to be **optimistic** and look for the good.

You can too.

My Top 5 Evolutionary Insights

1. Communicate, communicate, communicate!
2. Take time to reflect to make sure you are not redirecting to just one thing and overlooking other wonderful aspects that life offers.
3. Find what energises you and incorporate that into your life to perform at your best.
4. It's your choice how you respond to disappointment. Choose to be optimistic and look towards the future.
5. Find meaning in your life and the things that bring you happiness and joy.

"There is no path to happiness; happiness is the path."
"Happiness is a journey, not a destination."
(Buddha)

EIGHT

Breaking Free From Our Cocoon

*"It's ok to be a glow stick:
Sometimes we have to break before we shine."*
(Jadah Sellner)

What I told myself
This is a disaster. I have failed. I feel useless.
My body is fighting against me.
I hate my body. It's barren and not working.
Why did I get a body that does not work?
Why me? Why should I be the one to fail at something
so natural that everyone else can do?
I blame myself. This is my fault!

Failure, according to the Oxford Dictionary, is the lack of success in doing or achieving something. This is exactly how I felt. I was unable to do something that is innate to us as humans, something that I am expected to do and should be easy to do.

April 2008, 30 years after the first IVF baby was born and the year I turned 40, we stopped all forms of assisted reproductive therapy. That was it. I was childless and barren and had a party to signify not only my 40th but also the end of my dreams of being a mum.

It was a really hard day.

However, the moment that I realised I was definitely not going to be a mum was when I was told I was pre-menopausal and not when I ended IVF. This was due to all the stories you are told about people stopping their treatment and then becoming pregnant, and in the back of my mind, I always thought just maybe. In my heart, I held some miraculous hope that I may fall naturally. While I did not dwell on it as I had come to terms with living a life without kids, and I felt Al and I were enough, I was hopeful until it reached finality. Until that point, it was hard to accept that it was over.

I never thought that when we started the IVF process, we would not be successful. You read the information available, you hear about the success, but you don't hear about the failures. As I have mentioned several times throughout this book, no one talks about it not working, only how it worked. The books you read are about how to succeed, not what to do when you are unsuccessful. Many only share stories with happy endings rather than those with unhappy endings.

I blamed myself for a long time. I felt old, fat, and alone. Even though I had my amazing husband by my side, I still felt empty, and I did not know how I could change this. I felt like a huge failure, as I had failed my husband and my family.

Although I used to blame myself, I now realise that it is critical not to place blame on yourself or your partner. It's no one's fault; it is what it is, and you cannot change or control the situation or its outcome. It's important to forgive yourself—after all, you tried. Failing does not mean you cannot find happiness; it simply means you will explore other pursuits and different paths to joy. The sooner you accept this, the better it will be for everyone. This was a difficult realisation for me, and I won't pretend it was easy. I was the one with the issues, so it was easy to blame myself, which only added pressure to an already challenging situation.

You need to stop the self-hate talk. It will not help change the situation and will only negatively impact your emotional state. I had to be kind to myself. I asked myself what I would say to a family member or friend if they blamed themselves for something like this. I knew I would counter their negative self-talk, so I had to do the same for myself. However, you can't just turn off the desire to be a mum. It can feel incredibly lonely when you reach the end of this cycle of disappointment. It feels like you are paralysed. You may find yourself asking, "What do I do now?" and "Who do I talk to?" The resources available to support you through these situations are much better now than when I went through the process, but it would still be difficult to comprehend and find closure today.

Fertility treatment takes a significant toll on your body and health. By the end, I was overweight and very unhealthy, both emotionally and physically. This took some years to correct, and I have to say the weight stayed with me for the next ten years. This has now been rectified, but you need to be mindful of redirecting your grief into other pursuits, such as food, shopping, sports, or work.

During, and at the end of the cycle of disappointment, many around you will seem to fall pregnant at the drop of a hat (although, remember, it may not have been). This can be incredibly heartbreaking and presents one of the biggest challenges you might face. While you want to be genuinely happy for them, you are also grieving for your own situation, making it extremely difficult to process your own emotions. It's important to recognise this struggle, as this can be difficult to navigate. You want to be a good, supportive person, but you also find yourself thinking:

- Why them?
- Why not me?
- What's wrong with me?
- Why won't my body work?
- Am I broken?
- What is the reason I cannot do what feels natural and what everyone else seems to be able to do?

Given my circumstances, I tried to reassure myself that it was okay to feel this way. I acknowledged my feelings and let them out. Holding onto these emotions would have caused them to fester and made me dwell on them for longer than necessary. I also tried not to beat myself up for having these feelings, as that would have only worsened how I felt about myself. This was challenging because it's hard not to feel this way, which can make you feel like a bad person.

> **Be prepared for an outcome that changes all your life plans.**

You are not in control of the outcome, and the process is profoundly lonely and isolating. You think *"I will just do IVF and then will be a parent."* This may or may not be the case, as everyone is different, and you should not compare yourself to others. Some it works for, and some it does not. So be prepared for an outcome that changes all your life plans.

I learnt through this experience that failure is not a sign that we are less than others or not good enough. Not having children is not a failure; rather, it is a change in the direction of our lives. We can use this opportunity to reflect on our goals and decide where we want to direct our efforts. Maybe you are like me. I chose to focus my energy on leadership and helping others by sharing my experiences, which may be why this happened to me.

We all find fulfilment in different ways, and your way may be vastly different to mine. It's important to discover what your purpose is and how it resonates with you. Allow yourself to feel your emotions and be okay with them – do not let others tell you how you should feel. This is your journey, and that's important.

It will seem like one of the hardest things you will go through in your life, but remember, it could always be worse. We should celebrate what we have instead of dwelling on what we don't have.

Live the life you have.

How Others Feel

There are amazing individuals I know who are not parents and who are making remarkable contributions to their communities. They are achieving lifelong goals, fulfilling dreams, creating legacies and businesses, and building empires. They contribute to the world in extraordinary ways through the support they give to others and their personal achievements. This is how they choose to use their time and energy. However, it is important to note that this does not diminish what they would have accomplished if they were parents.

I have asked some of them how they felt now about not being a parent compared to how they felt in the past and whether they believe their lives are less fulfilled without kids of their own. I also asked them to reflect on the moment they realised they would not have kids.

Some found it hard to respond to this, but that's okay. We all experience grief in different ways, and while we lead fulfilled lives, we always feel the loss, which is important to acknowledge.

Some general responses are listed below, with some common themes, including feeling devastated, looking at other ways to lead fulfilling lives, and the need to consider how to navigate aging and who will provide support and care (or should I say who will be compelled to take care of them). For those of us without kids, these thoughts often occupy our minds. We frequently ask ourselves questions like, "Who will come and help fix stuff around the house that I can trust?" "Who will pick me up when I fall?" "Who will get me the essentials when I need them?" "Who will keep me company as I grow older?" It can be a very lonely place, and these concerns weigh heavily on our minds. However, despite these worries, many continue to lead happy and fulfilling lives.

Divorced Female

When her marriage ended in her late 30s, the grief associated with this was complicated by her thinking that now she would never be a mother; however, she could separate and minimise this grief with her own decision to undergo IVF using donor sperm. At that time, donor sperm was not available to single women in Victoria, and she had to travel to Canberra for treatment. Her desire to undertake this personal journey was so that she would never be left with the ultimate "what if?"

Whilst her first IVF implantation was initially successful, the pregnancy was not sustained to full term. With all the hormonal changes occurring with the miscarriage, it was a devastating loss for her. Her second implantation was unsuccessful; however, the disappointment was not as great. She had no further embryos, but her support network was very encouraging for her to attempt another cycle. She decided not to continue. She felt that this was the time when she realised she would not have children, although it ultimately became fact, like me, once she reached menopause. It was easier for her to make the decision not to continue the IVF process, as primarily, she is a fatalist. She strongly held the belief that if it was meant to be, it would have happened. She was no longer left with the "what if" as she had given it a try and was ultimately happy with her childless life.

With her decision to remain childless and create a new life for herself post-marriage breakdown, she put into place an earlier conceived plan to return to study, focusing on early childhood education. Since then, she has continued to work with vulnerable and at-risk children and has realised that there are more ways to provide "mothering" and have an impact on a child's life. And she also gets to live a life on her own terms. She is very comfortable with this and the fulfilling life she leads.

Married Couple
The couple had circumstantial infertility as they met late in life, and while they always wanted children, they could not. Adoption was considered, but in the end, they decided the process was not for them. They enjoy life and celebrate all it brings, and while they have struggled, they are fulfilled in what their life is now and look forward to the next round of adventures and travels. They often reflect on what is meant to be, will be. They do not dwell on this. They get on with life and all the challenges and joy it brings.

Male Same-Sex Couple
They always wanted kids, but their careers demanded a lot of time, energy, and focus. It just was not a priority for them at the time that would have enabled them to pursue

that path. Their only choice was going to be surrogacy, and this was a challenge, especially with COVID and travel issues. Adoption was also a consideration, but with the many rules and regulations in Australia, this isn't easy. Having looked into some of this and not wanting to be put through the scrutiny, they decided not to pursue this further. This was a tough time because they always saw themselves as being able to provide a loving and caring home for someone who really needed it.

When they realised that they were not going to have kids of their own, they felt incredibly sad as they had always pictured themselves having children, and they felt extremely disappointed.

Today, they have come to terms with not having their own kids and now, being in their mid-40s, they are becoming more involved with nieces and nephews and being part of their lives, which can be just as fulfilling for them. Also, this is convenient for them as they can always hand them back to their parents at the end of a long day.

One of their biggest worries is what happens as they age and who will visit them and take care of them if they get ill. There have been many discussions around coming together as friends and having their own retirement place with others in the same situation and some support staff around them.

Single Female
She has made several life choices that have given her some incredible life experiences and taken her around the world. She was so focused on travelling and using her education to excel in her career that she found it hard to prioritise relationships and put down deep roots. Even

now, she finds she does not tend to focus on her childless status. She feels it is more of a concern to others around her who believe her life isn't as complete as it should be.

She knows the likelihood of having children at her age is low, but she does not feel like it's totally impossible or that she couldn't consider adoption. She sometimes thinks about what it would feel like to be pregnant or daydream about what her future children might have looked like, but to her, it feels so alien. She also sees herself as a little old-fashioned and would only seek to be a parent if she found herself in a loving relationship, which she feels has also been a challenge in her life.

She has found genuine joy in sharing her siblings' experience with having children and has loved and embraced being an aunt. She finds it interesting to watch the difference time makes as the children get older and their personalities develop, but she cannot imagine how it really feels to be their birth parent. That said, she looks forward to supporting them, shaping their world through her storytelling, and being a trusted rock for them as they get older.

You can definitely get strength by connecting with others going through similar experiences.

∼

Being happy and fulfilled is a choice. You can either dwell on what you don't have or embrace and celebrate what you do have. Many, including myself, choose to embrace and celebrate what we have and smile. I choose to own all my challenges and accept everything that has happened to me, as it makes me who I am today. Every wrinkle from every tear is a part of me. I will embrace them all.

> *I choose to embrace and celebrate what I have and smile.*

Ongoing Grief

You grieve for all the experiences you will never have. I will never have the same experiences that others do when they have children, including moments that are often taken for granted or are an annoyance for some. The grief is real! And no, it's not the same doing or experiencing this with family or friends' kids. Don't get me wrong, it is extremely rewarding to be a part of this, but for me, it is not, and never will be, the same experience as doing these things with your own children.

Over time, we have experienced ebbs and flows of grief in various forms linked to different situations. Some of these situations have included:

- The parties and social gatherings that revolve around children.
- Christmas because it's a big reminder of what we don't have.
- Kids starting a school year and all the social media posts.
- Assumptions that we are not fully informed about the future or current topics or that we don't understand the love you have for a child unless you are a parent.
- Questions from others around: 'Do you have kids?'
- Questions about when you might become a grandmother?

In the first few years after stopping the treatment, I did not spend too much time looking at socials and all the posts, especially around the first day of school or first day of Kindergarten, Mother's Day or Father's Day, Christmas, and Easter.

While the grief has lessened, and the pain has become more manageable, it still lingers in the background.

∼

I find it interesting how I still struggle with my response when someone asks me if I am a mother or how many kids I have. I often reply to these questions with "none" or "I am not a mother," but I often feel compelled to justify this by adding, "but not by choice." I am not sure why I need to explain myself or why I even need to justify it. Maybe its because I don't want others to judge me or think I am selfish (not that I think those who don't have kids are) or that I put my career first. It's madness and something we put on ourselves. We need to stop putting this pressure on ourselves and stop assuming what others think.

During the process of trying to be a mum, my career was on hold (by choice) because I found it overwhelming. The process of trying to become a parent is not selfish; it's incredibly challenging, heartbreaking, and all-consuming. I still feel like some people judge you when you say you are not a mum or don't think you can be included in activities or discussions that they may want to have. However, this perception may not reflect reality; it may be just how I feel at times.

Forgive yourself; don't blame yourself.
You tried.

Whatever it is for you, please don't feel guilty or feel you need to justify it for others.

Given my experiences, I am now mindful of the questions I ask others about their lives, and while I don't always get it right, I reframe the questions. So instead of saying, "Do you have kids?" I ask the following questions.

So, who do you spend your time with?

Or

How do you spend your time?

These questions are more open and do not assume anything. They do not assume you are in a relationship, they do not assume you have kids, and they could be responded to in many ways—depending on how the person responding feels. For me, my answer to this would be my husband, my dog, my family, and my friends.

You could be childless for many reasons that are not by choice, including not meeting the right person to become a parent and missing the opportunity to even try. I am lucky to have my husband and to have been able to try.

Given my experience, I now focus on exploring various areas around this topic, especially in the workplace. I am passionate about not continuing to use terms like 'barren' or 'lonely cat ladies', especially with ourselves, when we refer to women who don't have partners or children, or both. I have been guilty of saying this about myself in the past. These terms are not aligned with how our communities are today. We comprise many diverse individuals with various lifestyles and family structures.

I believe people come in and out of our lives when we need them. I believe I was meant to undertake my journey so I could be here and guide others through their challenges. I have found strength in this belief, and it has made me realise how much I can fulfil my purpose and help those experiencing similar life-changing events with genuine empathy.

I needed to keep validating my beliefs, and you should too. You are courageous and strong, and your resilience will shine through and help you with your future challenges.

**Learn from these moments.
It's not a failure. It's a change of direction.**

My Top 5 Evolutionary Insights

1. You can thrive beyond this experience. You just need to break out of your cocoon.
2. You did not fail at anything; your life is destined to take a different path from what you envisioned.
3. Develop a purpose for yourself, and together, find what energises you.
4. Help to educate those that don't understand.
5. You need to let go of control; you cannot control everything.

"Failure is not the end of the road. It's a big red flag saying to you 'wrong way.' Turn around."
(Oprah Winfrey)

NINE

Embrace The Raindrops

Fly Like A Butterfly

"The way I see it, if you want the rainbow, you gotta put up with the rain."
(Dolly Parton)

What I told myself
What Now…
I am not a mum, but that will not define who I am.
I am still the same person I was before this started.
Maybe I am a bit broken, but deep down,
I am still the same.
I will do other things and have different adventures.
My life will be full of love, joy, and people.
I can focus on helping others.
There must be a reason why we have gone through this.

When you get to the end, stop and contemplate what this now means for you. For me, it was a mixture of guilt and relief. I felt relieved it was finally over and we could get on with our lives, and I felt guilty for feeling this way.

It felt like infertility had robbed us of the future we had wanted and imagined, and we mourned, and still do sometimes, for this loss, but… Creating a future that may be different but can be better is possible. We needed to leave our grief in the past, embrace what the future could be, and see what could be possible. This was an opportunity to create a life that may actually be better than we had imagined and may be as, or even more, fulfilling. We needed to get up from under the doona and believe anything was possible.

This was tough, but we did not give up and emerged stronger and more resilient. Although this part of our life was heartbreaking and debilitating, we created a new life that is exciting and rewarding most of the time.

These types of events in our lives can challenge our identities and aspirations. So, at the end of our cycle of disappointment, I had to ask myself – "Who would I be now? Who were we as a couple?" There were many questions, and we both needed to reflect on our new reality and determine what we wanted to become and achieve. We needed to be flexible since we were no longer going to be parents. What did this mean for us moving forward?

This was up to us.

> **We needed to embrace the new life we were going to have.**

We were in charge of our destiny, not anyone else, and certainly, no one else was going to tell us what we would be or do. What we knew was that we could not continue to dwell on what we had lost. We needed to embrace the new life ahead of us. I had to let go of the guilt and not allow it to define me; we needed to turn this situation into an opportunity for both of us. We explored alternative ways we could live and be, things we could do, and all the options we now had that would make this situation just a little bit more bearable.

Everyone is different, and everyone responds differently to challenging situations and outcomes. Still, we found that shifting our mindset and focusing on what we could control made it better for us and had less of an impact. In our own ways, we looked at the opportunities we could embrace, the life we would have, and all that we could pursue, try, and achieve. We did not want to give up on life because of this situation, nor did we want to retreat from the world. We wanted our lives back, and we wanted to embrace the world and all the opportunities it could give us. We needed to show up and live again.

During difficult times, it's important to accept your situation and understand the possibilities of what your life could be, even while you still feel the pain. To do this, you may need support, so seek out that help, whether through psychological support or through friends and family—whatever works best for you—but you need to try. We did. For me, it was talking about it with my family and friends, but I also immersed myself in learning more and focusing on my career. We realised that we could not stay where we were as we felt this would slow our healing process.

And at the end of the journey, it's important to mark it with something. We bought a boat! This was a way of saying goodbye to that potential life and hello to a new one. We felt it was necessary to shed our old life and fully embrace the new one. Even if we stumbled on our way there, it was better than staying where we were. We understood that we had to let go of the past and what we had desired to enable us to fully embrace what the future could be.

I've come to realise that even in times of significant loss and grief, when everything feels chaotic and confusing, there's a chance to create a new and exciting life. Embrace this and explore all the options. Experiment, be creative, and consider everything that comes your way.

You need to accept the reality of your situation and then move forward toward a very different path. Look at the good times, even in the bad times; laugh when you can, and allow yourself to experience happiness and joy. Acknowledge your feelings, whether they are good or bad. I focused on one, two, or three good things that happened during the week, even while I was grieving. This is how we got through this time. It is possible to feel happiness and find purpose while feeling as though you'll never come out of your grief. Allow yourself time to grieve, but also allow yourself time to feel happiness and laughter.

I found joy and happiness in my relationship with Al, my friends, family, art, learning, photography, and travel. We were creating lifelong experiences, and I discovered what energises me and makes me happy.

I can now look at my life and say yes, sometimes we are selfish when we choose not to go on holidays when there might be lots of kids there (because we don't have to), and we don't attend every kid's event. Don't get me wrong, we support all our wonderful family and friends' kids and will be there at the drop of a hat if needed, but we don't feel the need to participate in all the activities that a family with kids enjoys or does. Sometimes, we prefer to do other things we enjoy and not feel guilty about it. That is one benefit of not being a parent yourself. We don't need kids around us all the time to feel fulfilled. We just need to live our best life, and sometimes that means not always doing everything everyone else is doing. That's okay, and your family and friends should understand this. We know ours do.

Appreciate what you have now and be content and happy with that. Anything else will be a bonus.

There is a word called 'Santosha', and when I heard it, its meaning resonated with me. It means 'completely content and satisfied' and has a history in Indian philosophy along with connections to yoga practices (not that I practise yoga; I am way too uncoordinated). I hadn't felt content or satisfied for some time, so it was very timely when I stumbled across this word and its meaning. 'San' means 'to be completely, entirely,' and 'Tosha' is 'contentment, satisfaction, acceptance.' Together, this means 'to be completely content with or satisfied within the moment.'

To me, this means that we can find complete satisfaction and contentment in our lives right now. We can accept and appreciate what we have and who we are. By reminding ourselves that we are enough, both individually and together, we can move forward and focus on appreciating what we do have rather than dwelling on what we don't have. We should find satisfaction in the present instead of constantly searching for fulfilment and contentment outside our current circumstances or in areas we cannot control. We can celebrate and embrace what we have in the present moment and be grateful for everything in our lives today. I found that adopting this mindset has made our lives happier and more content, reducing our longing for what we could not have. While we still have aspirations and goals associated with what we want to do and achieve, we appreciate the 'now.' This way of thinking has helped me find peace and contentment with what I have in the moment.

Being a parent is not the only way you can be happy or content. Focus on what you have right now; be content and find joy in that. Everything else will be a bonus. It's important to work towards your happiness, both now and in the future.

For me, it was important to remove the view that I could not be content or happy without kids. Once I did this, I discovered that I had a pretty incredible life with some great opportunities and that I was in a position to give back to others, as well as have time to learn and grow myself. I needed to ensure that the stories I was telling myself were accurate and reflected who I was and still am, not what I thought I should be or what I wanted in the future.

Don't miss out on the now by trying to find the future that may not be as you envisage.

It was crucial to ensure we were doing things throughout this process that gave us something to look forward to. Some of these include taking up a hobby, planning a trip, splurging on myself, enjoying a good pampering session, enjoying a long lunch, or having a long relaxing breakfast. There are many ways to make yourself feel better, especially when you're feeling sad or angry. Personally, I found motivation through various pursuits, such as learning something new, seeing people succeed, painting, having fun whenever possible, and laughing until it hurts. Travel has also become a large part of our lives. For me, travel has always been important, both before and after IVF. I love to travel and seize every opportunity I get. Now we have the freedom to travel whenever we want, without any restrictions.

Creating My Purpose

It was vital for me to create a purpose and vision for my life, allowing me to envisage a future I wanted to create. I crafted a purpose so I had something to focus on and look forward to.

The purpose I have created for my life is to help others. My goal is to improve the lives of those around me and make them more fulfilling.

In developing my purpose, I reflected on several key questions: Who do I want to impact? How will I achieve this? What am I striving for? What do I want from my life? I realised I could pursue anything I desired, but it was essential to understand what was motivating me; this needed to be clear.

In defining my purpose, I considered what matters most to me beyond just having children. I reflected on my strengths and passions, what gives me joy and what energises me and how to use these to build a purpose and give back to others. This process helped me discover my purpose. I aspire to achieve my purpose and work towards it daily—in my job, with my family, as a friend, and as a leader. This motivates me to get out of bed every day.

∽

**My purpose is to help others.
It is to make the lives of those around me
better and more fulfilled.**

In the long run, not being a parent means you can have more freedom, more time, more money (once your IVF journey is over and maybe if you don't buy a boat 😊), more choice around how and where you live, more travel and more flexibility. This is not to say you cannot have these things as a parent—you absolutely can—but without children, these decisions and activities only require two of you to decide, or just you, depending on your circumstances. From my perspective, children do not make you who you are or what you can achieve, they enhance your life and give you different experiences.

Being Grateful Everyday

I have a fulfilling career where I have worked for some great organisations that have given me countless opportunities. I have led amazing people and seen them grow and create their own fulfilment, both with and without families. I have studied what and when I wanted to, I connect regularly with family and friends, and I have travelled the world. We have had great adventures where we saw and had once-in-a-lifetime experiences. We have amazing and wonderful family and friends around us. And all this is what fulfils me and makes me grateful every day.

A gratitude journal helped me reflect on the good things, as small as they were, as a lot of small things can add up to something bigger, and this helped.

Some of the things I am grateful for that give me joy and fulfilment are:

- My husband.
- My Dogs.
- My Family and friends.
- Learning something new.
- My career opportunities.
- Sleeping in on a Sunday.
- Brunch.
- Long lunches.
- Networking and socialising.
- Gold Class and watching a movie in luxury with a cocktail in my hand.
- Wine and cocktails with friends.
- A live band.
- Dancing like no one is watching.
- Singing like no one is listening (my go-to is Jessie's Girl).

- Sitting with the dog under a tree and a glass of my favourite wine in hand.
- Painting and getting caught up in the moment where you actually slow down.
- Feeling the sun on my body.
- Feeling the grass under my bare feet.
- Being outdoors in the fresh air.
- Being in water.
- Meditating.
- Binge watching TV.

> **My life is fulfilled in ways that make me happy, and yours will be too.**

Every story and every journey is different, and mine differs from Al's. What we all have in common is that we are going through, or have gone through, something that is a real struggle we all need to process in our own way, which has different outcomes for everyone.

What worked for me, and my guidance to anyone going through this, is to focus on all the good in your life and practice gratitude for it. Don't focus on what you don't have. My glass is half full, not half empty. I regularly reflect on my life, the people in it, and what I have achieved already. It is important to stop and reflect on this. This is something I will continue to do. I focus on the areas in my life and the people that add value and make me happy.

You need to find something to smile at. Even in the worst imaginable situation, Al and I still tried to find something to make us smile. It isn't easy, but it is possible. Use humour to counter the ridiculous things people say, journal how you feel, and do things that bring you joy.

Even if you are not a parent, you can still lead a fulfilling life. Life goes on and can still be rewarding, and you can have several remarkable aspects to your life, even if being a parent is not one of them. Enjoy your life, and don't waste it by worrying about what you don't have.

It takes time to heal, and on your journey to healing, you will come across things that trigger you. It's critical you focus on what you have and where you are headed. Some may never understand this unless they have walked a similar path to you.

Critical to my life now is to ensure we consider the 'what if' scenarios, as we now know that plans can change at any moment. I also needed to look at what was around me to avoid missing great opportunities by just focusing on one outcome.

Today, my life is fulfilling in ways that make me happy; yours will be too.

My Top 5 Evolutionary Insights

1. See the world, embrace the raindrops, and fly like a butterfly.
2. Your happiness should not be defined by what you want, but by what you have.
3. Think about your Plan B and find other meanings in your life.
4. Plan for your future. Ask yourselves what your life could look like without children and what your aspirations are beyond this.
5. Don't put your life on hold. Identify future possibilities to help you move forward.

"When life throws you a rainy day, play in the puddles."
(Winnie the Poo)

TEN

Why Don't We Talk About It?

Leadership And Vulnerability

"Try to be a rainbow in someone else's cloud."
(Maya Angelou)

What I told myself
What do you mean, no one talks about it?
I need to talk about it openly as a leader.
We need to talk about it. If we don't, how will we support others?
Why do people say this makes me courageous?
We should just share for others.
Let's help others in this situation.

The challenge of the cycle of disappointment is that it gives you no other choice but to stall your career.

It is almost impossible to do it all.

I was always career-oriented, and even if I were to become a mum, I would do both. My life was never just about being a mum. Even so, this does not change how hard this process has been for me.

I have worked hard and continue to develop my career and leadership capabilities, and I have been fortunate to have had many opportunities along the way. While there has always been a hole that cannot be filled, I can honestly say that I feel fulfilled throughout my life, even with other challenges we currently face.

I have always wanted it all and believed I could have it all. I wanted to meet the man of my dreams, be a wife and a mum, and have a successful career. I feel it is vital that we recognise you don't always get it all. If you don't get it all, it does not make you any less of a person. To be honest, who really gets it all and gets it all at the same time anyway? I have seen many sacrifices made over the years, especially by women who think they need to prove they can have it all and do it all. This is simply not sustainable.

WHY DON'T WE TALK ABOUT IT?

Let's stand up, talk about not having it all, and spread the word that it is okay. We don't always get it all!

#idonthaveitall #itsokIdonthaveitall #youwillbeok #letsmakeitnormal

---

You are strong, resilient, and fabulous, so don't ever forget that.

We hear about and celebrate those who have successful careers, are amazing parents, and live a steady and stable life without worries or issues. Or do they? In today's era of social media, we are bombarded daily with these images and posts. However, I want to remind you that we don't all get it all, or maybe we just can't have it all at the same time, and that's okay. We experience other aspects of our lives that are valuable and rewarding. Social media tends to present the most romanticised version of ourselves and our lives. We go through life facing setbacks and challenges, and for each of us, these are different and unique, but these experiences make us who we are.

As leaders, we need to be open about our experiences and let others know we all have struggles, and that's normal. Let's be our authentic selves. We need to be comfortable talking openly about it. We need to normalise the discussion, be vulnerable, and move away from it feeling taboo.

Perhaps fertility is a taboo subject because when we discuss fertility or trying to have a baby, it is about sex, and people don't like to discuss sex. Is this why?

As women, our careers start and end hormonally.

From puberty and menstruation through to getting pregnant, or trying to get pregnant, to menopause, we need to talk about it, and as leaders, we need to be okay with that.

As women, our professional journey can be impacted by our hormonal challenges. Our careers start and end hormonally. In the first part of our careers, we might struggle with painful and challenging menstruation cycles, good, bad, and ugly, and then move on to finding a partner (if we want to and can) before trying to get pregnant. If this is not easy, it can be a challenging time for all. Even if we are successful, we may experience issues with the pregnancy or even with our children, along with the difficulties of family life (life is not always smooth). You finally reach the other end of your career, and you encounter menopause.

The hormones never stop flowing.

It's not easy to get on every day.

It's not easy to stay focused on your career.

It's also not easy for the partner supporting this.

As a woman facing these emotional and hormonal challenges throughout your career, it will and does impact how you bring yourself to work. It's crucial that we have conversations to normalise this. These discussions will also help those supporting their partners through these pivotal moments.

You go through life and expect to have kids, and even when going through IVF, you still expect to come out the other side successfully. I want to enable the conversation to support others and let them know they are not alone and that the support is there throughout their careers.

As a leader, I share my story, showing this vulnerable side of me. This has enabled those around me in the workplace and beyond to feel comfortable enough to share their own stories. My openness has made me someone others feel at ease talking to. I speak to many who are experiencing these issues throughout their careers, and I try to guide and support them through the process, letting them know that what they feel and experience is normal. I share my journey and talk about what I did and what worked for me. While I am aware that what worked for me may not work for all, I am hopeful that sharing what helped in my situation may inspire others with ideas to help in theirs.

There needs to be more discussion about how people can be supported in the workplace during pivotal, challenging times in their lives. It's crucial that assumptions are not made about someone suggesting they are just being emotional, difficult, or overreacting; there may be other challenges at play. As leaders, we need to lean in to understand what is impacting them.

It is critical that reproductive issues and childlessness are formally addressed in the workplace.

Workplace Challenges

In 2020, a Fertility Matters at Work survey highlighted the fertility-related challenges individuals experienced in the workplace. The results indicated that 61% of respondents did not feel confident in talking to their employer about attempting to conceive, and over 68% of respondents believed that their treatment significantly impacted their mental and emotional well-being. Along with this, 25% of respondents reported having negative experiences with their employer during this time.[49] With 1 in 6 individuals affected by medical infertility, it is crucial to address these challenges within the workplace. I found it extremely challenging to navigate this cycle of disappointment whilst getting up every day to show up and deliver quality work.

Research conducted by MIST Workshops Ltd, an organisation that provides training and support for workplaces on reproductive issues and childlessness, highlights that employees who are facing these challenges often feel ostracised at work. In fact, 85% of affected employees reported feeling triggered by pro-natal practices at work, such as pregnancy announcement emails; 76% reported receiving insensitive comments; and 64% expressed fear of discrimination when disclosing their miscarriage or infertility at work. Furthermore, 72% did not even inform their workplace about their situation.[50,51]

There needs to be a better understanding of the energy required to balance infertility treatment and work.

I remember all the challenges and issues I faced while navigating various parts of my journey, and I didn't know how to manage them or feel that anyone would understand. This included the times I needed to attend appointments and recover from procedures I had undergone, with the timing of these never being work-friendly. Additionally, I dealt with the emotional and financial pressures of holding back my career, not performing at my best, and constantly worrying about the costs associated with my treatment.

There needs to be a greater understanding of the energy required to balance fertility treatment and work from both male and female perspectives, each as challenging as the other. Throughout this time, anything in life that is non-essential is put on hold. I am sure many are reluctant to change roles or move companies during this time for fear of losing maternity or paternity benefits. As a result, they often stay in their jobs and positions where they are unhappy and may disengage, which only adds to the pressure.

I stayed in my role longer than I intended despite not being fully satisfied and wanting to expand my career. The fear of change and 'just in case' was why I did not move. This fear of change and 'just in case' thinking hindered my progress.

Financial stability is another key aspect of fertility treatment, which can lead you to hold onto a role or stay in an organisation that may not be the best for you. Changing your job and company mid-process would only add additional unnecessary pressure and stress.

I found it was important to share my challenges with those closest to me at work, as well as with my leader. If there is one time in your career when you need additional support, it's at this time, whether you are the person going through it or you are supporting your partner through it. Talk about it and share it with those around you so they understand what is happening and can provide the right level of support, to make your journey easier, with fewer distractions and less pressure placed on yourself.

I remember being at work, just trying to get through meetings without breaking down and wanting to walk out or yell at someone. I was angry and sad, and no one understood what I was going through.

When I went through it, there were no honest discussions about it anywhere because no one spoke up. Today, it is promising to see increased openness. However, we still shy away from openly discussing some of these pivotal challenges, like menstruation, post-natal depression, infertility, and menopause, just to name a few. We need to remove the stigma associated with these topics, especially in our workplaces where people spend most of their time. Not discussing these areas in the workplace is no longer ok. How you bring yourself to work, to a negotiation, or to a relationship with colleagues, peers, and stakeholders can be influenced by what you are experiencing outside of work and how you show up.

We spend a significant portion of our lives at work. So it is crucial we get support and understanding during life-changing situations.

Fertility challenges can have a significant impact on those going through it and those supporting them. We need to get these challenges out and in the open, provide a safe environment for people to share them, and provide the right support, ensuring they are not perceived negatively or associated with performance discussions. We spend a significant portion of our lives working, and we require the right support and understanding when going through such life-changing situations. If your workplace cannot support you during this time, it is critical you find one that will. It's important that the workplace provides a safe and secure environment where everyone feels supported to discuss these topics without fear of being treated differently.

The impact that work pressure, stress, and fertility have on mental health, and well-being highlights the importance of supporting our people through these challenges and creating a psychologically safe place for people to thrive, regardless of external issues they may be facing.

In many workplaces, there is a focus on families, births and pregnancy, providing various channels of support and celebration around these topics. However, we still don't see infertility as highly visible and openly spoken about. I know in my discussions that some feel if they share this part of their life, it will have a negative impact on their career and hold them back. Being able to share your personal difficulties in the work environment provides greater support for you and greater ability for the organisation to support you. It is encouraging and inspiring to see more leaders displaying vulnerable and authentic leadership by sharing how they are feeling and just being human - but we still have a way to go.

We are also now seeing an increasing number of studies and publications regarding infertility and the impact that it has in the workplace, and this is now shining the light on one of many issues faced by people who go to work every day. One study in 2022 by Manchester Metropolitan University identified two key areas of concern. The first was the vast difference in experiences individuals had at work, including the differences in the level of comfort people felt when discussing their infertility, how management and colleagues responded, and how this resulted in either a positive or negative impact. The second finding revealed that most organisational policies and responses were not sufficiently helpful, specifically around management support and knowledge. Recommendations from this report, in the context of work, included raising awareness, peer support, management training and further development of policies.[52]

In addition to the various studies, publications and the work being done by WHO, I was pleased to see the Harvard Business Review released a paper in November 2020 entitled "Employers, It's Time to Talk About Infertility."[53] In this paper, they suggested that the workplace challenges experienced by those going through this difficult time included the fear that informing their organisations would have a negative effect on their careers, preventing them from receiving the right level of support and understanding throughout the process. There is a call in this paper for business leaders to discuss this issue openly and implement policies that will support their people during all phases of their infertility process.

∽

Given the human right to have a child and its link to the UN SDGs, as well as the recognition of infertility as a prevalent disease, it is time for organisations to review their policies and the support networks available for their employees regarding infertility and fertility treatments. Most organisations are now aligning their policies with the UN SDGs, so it is timely for this discussion topic to be included.

Health and well-being education and discussions are increasingly being integrated into the workplace, something I believe COVID has contributed to by blurring the line between work and home. This is creating a safer place for people, including leaders, to be more transparent and open about their struggles and life outside of work. This is critical to ensure those going through a process know they are not alone and that they will be ok.

While we have made significant progress in the workplace, there are still some areas that need to be considered. For example, we cater very well for people with children. However, we do not cater for or often discuss those without children or those who are struggling to have them. We provide parental leave, family-friendly policies, childcare, and Christmas leave. But we don't really consider what else we need to do to support those who may not be parents, the childless and the circumstantial, involuntarily childless.

It seems like we are always focused on, or perceived to be focused on, families, especially during holidays, as well as work policies and initiatives. For those of us without kids, we often struggle with these policies and initiatives. We hear in the language used that they only apply if you have kids. While I know that this is not how most organisations view these types of policies, we need to ensure that we are clear and inclusive in the language we use and how we classify families. For example, our dog is our family. For others, it could be a fish, a bird or a close friend. It is the individual who has the relationships and, therefore, defines who forms part of their family. So, with this in mind, are work policies clear enough to prevent individual managers from deciding whether our pets or close friends can be considered family? I don't think they are.

We also need to ensure that we are not inadvertently overlooking various groups who are not parents due to their unique circumstances. We need to stop creating policies that focus on the success of these journeys and instead consider how we can redesign them to support those who have faced setbacks or who are child-free. For instance, we could extend parental leave and integration back into the workplace after a successful birth to those who are returning after experiencing a pregnancy loss.

Infertility can affect anyone, regardless of gender, sexual orientation, or ethnicity, and how individuals cope with their infertility may vary considerably. It is crucial to use inclusive language and represent all individuals and their various pathways to parenthood within the workplace through implementing policies, education, internal support networks, and raising awareness. We need to create a greater understanding of fertility and its challenges with respect to people's health and well-being, the LGBTQ+ community, intersectionality with cultural challenges, alternative pathways to parenthood and alternative family structures.

We need to consider how employers can create more inclusive narratives to ensure there is support for all as part of overall diversity strategies.

"Diversity is being asked to the party, inclusion is being asked to dance."
(Verna Myers)

I found during my journey that it was difficult to operate at my best and at the level I wanted to. I placed a lot of unnecessary pressure on myself because I perceived this as taboo, and I did not think at the time that I could openly discuss it with many people at work. One of the hardest moments was balancing workloads with multiple appointments and tests, along with my raging hormones from all the drugs.

Some of the aspects that workplaces are now implementing, or should consider implementing, include:

- Fertility and menstruation-friendly policies, enabling leave without scrutiny.
- Leave for loss and surrogacy situations.

- Infertility and fertility-informed policies with extra time off for preconception, reduced hours and responsibilities, counselling, and financial support.
- Understanding treatments and their spontaneity, along with the need that you may not have a choice but to drop everything and go.
- Not having it linked to parental leave.
- To enable extended leave for miscarriage, irrespective of what stage of pregnancy it occurs.
- Improved information and education for leaders and managers to enable them to understand the impact of infertility, navigate the conversations, and provide the right level of support.
- Understanding the emotional outbursts that may happen without being judged by them.
- Greater flexibility regarding where and how the work is done–working from home would be a great support for many during this time.
- Normalise it by enabling discussions and using the terminology.
- Infertility as a disease should enable personal leave to be more readily accessible.
- Flexibility to enable treatments and appointments to be attended during working hours.
- Career planning flexibility programmes to get back on track when ready, regardless of the outcome, or to continue to pursue treatment.
- Removal of pregnancy wait times.

As leaders, we need to be open about our situations and challenges, drive the right initiatives and policies, and ensure our organisations are having meaningful discussions and supporting all people regardless of their challenges.

I think it is time to break the silence and share our journeys to remove the stigma around these medical problems and help others understand. This will ensure that others going through their infertility journey in the workplace can receive the support and encouragement they need without feeling like I did. That's my mission. I want these subjects to stop being taboo in the workplace and to be openly discussed, to normalise the challenge and help others feel less isolated.

Not being a mum meant I needed to redirect my natural nurturing instincts into my career. Through this, I hope I have helped and supported many people along the way. My purpose in my career is to help others learn and grow while they work with me, to enable them to move onto what and where they need to be, with or without me.

This is what drives me.

I lead with vulnerability, sharing my journey and talking about what got me here, what makes me who I am and how this has helped me. My journey has enabled me to build greater resilience and has encouraged me to maintain an optimistic outlook, seeing the good in all aspects of my life rather than focusing on what's missing. It has helped me to develop a sense of gratitude in my life. I apply what I have learnt from my experiences to how I help others.

Working with and mentoring others allows me to apply what I have learnt and share my experiences. I support them as they navigate the difficulties in their life, whether it is infertility or other challenges they may be facing related to fertility, which are often silent and invisible.

As a leader, when supporting anyone facing trauma, loss, or stress, we also need to be mindful of how we respond to those experiencing these challenges. Even with the best intentions, we can get it wrong if we do not fully understand what the individual is going through. Therefore, it's important we speak out as leaders about the challenges that have affected our lives so people have someone to turn to, who they know will truly understand their situation.

It's also vital that we are mindful about giving advice if we don't really understand a person's situation. Even when we do understand, we need to be mindful that we are only offering information based on our journey, which will be different to theirs.

I have gained a vast amount of knowledge throughout my leadership journey.

I have learnt…

- I'm the one who has the power to determine my actions and how I respond to various challenges.
- Making others successful and supporting them gives me joy.
- To be a role model for others and share my story.
- You need to create healthy habits and increase your awareness.
- To practice vulnerability, excellence, resilience, and kindness.
- To be my authentic self.
- To choose the attitude I bring to work.
- To be the CEO of my own career.
- To have real connections and real conversations.
- To always act with integrity.

- To own my mistakes.
- To enable people rather than direct and control them.
- To lead with purpose and passion.
- Mentoring others is valuable.
- To invest in myself and learn new things.
- To have good networks, these are important, and you need to invest time in building them.
- To take myself out of my comfort zone to cultivate my growth and development.
- It is important to provide a safe place to share personal journeys, both good and bad.
- To be informed about what others are going through.
- Those you lead need to know they will be supported, or they will be reluctant to tell you.
- You cannot help everyone, but you can share your experiences to enable others to feel comfortable to share with you.

> **As a leader and a colleague, you need to bring your whole self to work.**

As leaders, we need to stop trying to be perfect and just be authentic. We can use our experiences to thrive and enable our people to thrive. As a leader and a colleague, you need to bring your whole self to work. We are all just human, after all, and everyone has something challenging happening in their lives.

Also, leaders need to be the catalyst for change rather than sitting back and waiting for organisations to change. We are the organisation, so it is up to us to be the voice of those who feel they may not have a voice. There were a lot of elements I struggled with, so I feel I need to be the voice for others and champion the discussion now.

Most people face struggles and issues, and maybe we just don't share them because we don't want people to think we are weak or we don't want them to affect our careers. However, keeping these to ourselves can make others feel isolated and alone with their struggles.

There are excellent resources available now to help you navigate the infertility discussion in the workplace and get the support you need. What has been encouraging to see are various groups focusing on this issue, including Fertility Matters at Work, a Community Interest Company dedicated to improving fertility support at work and ensuring fertility is recognised and supported across all organisations. Additionally, MIST Workshops Ltd is an organisation that provides support for workplaces on reproductive issues, including pregnancy loss, infertility, and childlessness. We need more organisations like these, given the prevalence of infertility.

Most people are experiencing or have experienced something challenging. Sharing demonstrates courage and honesty when you put yourself out there - the good, the bad and the challenging.

My Top 5 Evolutionary Insights

1. Don't be afraid to share your challenges. You will discover that you are not alone and many others are going through similar challenges.
2. It's okay to say you need help.
3. Utilise work employee assistance programs and tools when you need to. Speak up if they are unavailable.
4. If you cannot share with your leader or manager, find someone who you trust and confide in them.
5. Don't hesitate to reach out if someone shares their journey; this alone will help you navigate your journey.

"As you grow older, you will discover you have two hands, one for helping yourself, the other for helping others."
(Audrey Hepburn)

ELEVEN

What Next...

New Challenges And Life Beyond

"Being challenged in life is inevitable, being defeated is optional."
(Roger Crawford)

What I told myself

Surely, we cannot have another life-changing event happen.
Why does this happen to us?
We can navigate this and find a way; we are stronger together and can get through anything.
Life is full of challenges, and we need to navigate through them together.

It is how we choose to respond that is the key to happiness.

While my life is fulfilled, and I embrace the concept of Santosha, there will always be something else that comes along and knocks you off your feet. After all, that is life, and it has its ups and downs. How we choose to respond is the key to happiness. We can choose to wallow in all that is wrong, or we can choose to embrace what is good, celebrate that, and deal with the challenging aspects in a calm and controlled way, focusing on each step as it comes.

My husband Al has been a great influence on me as we navigate each issue in our lives in the moment. He is optimistic and deals with each situation in the best way he can at the time.

There are many heartbreaking moments we will experience in our lifetime, and infertility is one of them. However, we refuse to let it completely define who we are. We have faced the loss of loved ones, and various incidents have happened to us and our family and friends over the years, and this will continue. What we do with those experiences and how we choose to live beyond them is what matters most to us.

WHAT NEXT...

No matter how prepared we think we are, we need to find resilience to enable us to adapt to the various situations that present themselves. For us, resilience has come from this journey, and now we are faced with the next challenge. There is one constant in life: it will always present you with other challenges to focus on or overcome. Life has many moments for everyone that are difficult, whether you experience loss, illness, heartache, health and well-being issues, or just loneliness. There can be heartbreaking instances with people dying far too young and various other tragic incidents taking place.

With resilience comes the ability to adapt, be flexible, and tackle all the challenges life throws at you, and there will be more. To me, resilience is a skill you can build by refusing to let challenges bring you down and ensuring you emerge from these challenging situations with minimal change to who you are and greater knowledge to share. While our life has had many ups and downs, we now face more issues that have tested us and our resolve.

Illness

In 2017, my husband Al began to get sick. He tried to push through with life, but as each month passed, this became harder and harder. He spoke to multiple doctors and specialists and has researched many possibilities himself.

He has been told it could be many different afflictions, but it turns out to be none of those. He gets different doctors disagreeing with each other's diagnosis, and he has undergone about 1,000 tests, with many being inconclusive or have ruled out what was being investigated. This whole process has required us to be highly resilient and for Al to stay optimistic with each test.

As I write this book, he is still undergoing further tests. While there are various diagnoses, they are all still being evaluated by various specialists. We even joked that he needs a specialist for all his specialists. He is one of the most optimistic people I know, and he just gets on with it, even without the ability to really live his life to the fullest.

Al has never held me back from doing what I love and has consistently encouraged me to pursue all I want. With this he encourages me to continue to lead my life in a way that brings me happiness. He encourages me to pursue all the adventures and activities I enjoy doing, including writing this book, studying, and travelling with friends and family. He also keeps me grounded when I need that.

My hope for him is that we receive a clearer diagnosis and find therapies that help ease his discomfort and enable him to regain his life and live it to the full again.

This is life, and it could be worse. We are blessed in so many ways, and this is just another challenge that tests us as a couple and as individuals.

We are strong and remain strong, and we will get through this next challenge. While our life together is different now, with Al's limited ability to join me in all social events and travels, we are still very much in love and extremely supportive of each other. We do life together, which includes the hard stuff. We will not run as soon as it gets hard. We will stick together through it all and emerge stronger and happier in the end.

As I write this, our dog Bear is now 6 years old. He is a red heeler and a massive handful. He brings us joy and laughter and is a little crazy. The nickname we gave him as a puppy was "Crazy Bear." We have called him many names, but this is the only name I can share in this book!

Unfortunately, he fell quite ill as a puppy, which resulted in two extended stays at the vet. Ever since he has needed a special diet and cannot eat many foods. Although he loves to eat a stick or kangaroo poo! He brings us so much joy even though he has his issues.

Ironically, part of the medication he is on is similar to Al's, which is amusing considering what they say—our pets often resemble us, not only in looks but also in their behaviour.

I have two sick boys at home who struggle most days. I often look at this and wonder, is this the reason we didn't have our own children? Is it because it would have been an even bigger battle for us with kids in this environment?

While no one, including me, can fully understand what it's like to be in Al's body, we can at least seek to understand.

~

Being Grandparents

We will not be grandparents, which was an unexpected realisation. When I went through the grieving process, I did not contemplate that I would not be a grandmother. At the time of realising I would never be a mum, the reality of not being a grandmother or Al not being a grandfather had not crossed my mind.

Not being a parent, you move on with a different life and don't dwell too much on what you don't have. You focus on what you have, and then another challenge comes out of the blue.

At the time we went through our process, no one spoke about these other areas of life you would not experience either; you just did not think about it. But the reality is that you are also not going to be a grandparent, and that is another grieving process you need to go through.

Aging Without Children

The other challenge for those of us without children is the feeling of apprehension about what will happen to us as we age. While most of us have children in our lives through family and friends, it is definitely different from having our own. This means we need to consider what we do as we age, as there may not be anyone around we can automatically rely on to look after us. I know most people say, 'but your nieces and nephews will', but I don't think it is fair to rely on this automatically happening. Additionally, many argue that it's not guaranteed, even with kids. However, I believe most of those around us would definitely have their children look after them as they age.

The next phase is for us to plan our future and envision what it might look like for us. It is important to navigate this and have a plan, even if we know the plan may change. Maybe our nieces and nephews will take care of us; maybe we will move to a retirement community. Alternatively, our friends who are in a similar situation might create a support network together. There are many options to consider and explore, but our family and friends are loving, and we know they will always be there, no matter what. It's not something we need to worry about now, but it is an important consideration when planning for our future.

We will implement strategies to ensure we have the right support when and where we need it. I like the idea of a retirement location with others and a community around us, with our friends and family in similar situations.

My Top 5 Evolutionary Insights

1. How you react to what happens to you can define how you can move beyond it. You are in control of your reactions and responses to challenges.
2. Be Optimistic. Glass is half full.
3. Don't dwell on what you don't have; embrace what you have.
4. Try to find positivity in the future based on what you have rather than what you don't have.
5. Living is about accepting the good with the bad. It's up to you how you react.

"We cannot direct the wind, but we can adjust the sails."
(Dolly Parton)

TWELVE

Evolutionary Insights

*"Live as if you were to die tomorrow.
Learn as if you were to live forever."*
(Mahatma Gandhi)

What I told myself
I learnt so much.
I need to share what I have learnt.
Even if I can help one person, I have to share.
Sometimes, we don't get it all!

I was once asked, "What makes you optimistic?"

I responded, *"Meeting, working with and leading passionate, motivated people makes me optimistic."*

Reflecting on this, I can see how it has played out in my life and during challenging times. I recognise how blessed I am to have been surrounded by positive people, both in my private life and in my work life. I now understand how this has helped me get through tough moments. Being optimistic has, and will continue to, allow me to remain hopeful about life and all it can bring.

I found it essential to reflect on what happened to me and create my own narrative rather than run away from it; I am grateful for what I learnt and how I can use this to help others. This enables me to choose what values and lessons I take from the experience.

Throughout our lives, we will be confronted with many difficulties that can divert us from the path we believed we were on. While we cannot control these events, we can control how we respond to them. It's important that we create new narratives for our lives and not cling to what we planned, what we thought we wanted, or what has happened in the past. I have learnt that our lives never follow a straight line or particular order. We can plan it all out, but we do not have full control over the eventual outcome.

I gained resilience and learnt how to deal with aspects of life that were not always going to plan. I realised I cannot control everything as much as I would like, but I always have another plan to focus on or a plan that can be changed as things evolve.

I need to accept that I cannot predict or control the future. I need to explore and discover other possibilities I can pursue and aim for in my life.

It is essential to recognise positivity and happiness in the small things you do every day, like spending time with family and friends, cooking a meal for someone else, reading a book, listening to a podcast, achieving something at work, binge-watching a series, painting or just hanging out under the tree with your pet. There are many things you can do to help you find joy and happiness every day.

For those of you who are mums, please never feel guilty for having something that some of us cannot. Cherish every moment, and when things are tough, acknowledge the hard times and consider how you would feel if your kids were not around. Some of us would love to experience what you do.

I choose to live an optimistic, happy and fulfilled life, even if it is different to what I imagined.

My story is my own, and by sharing my experiences, I hope to provide insight into the challenges of infertility and how you can mentally prepare to start to rediscover yourself and live a fulfilling life, celebrating all that you have and all that you will have. Life is a constant navigation where we cannot always control what happens to us, but we can control how we respond.

Would I have had kids earlier if I had known I had issues? Maybe not. I was never ready until I met Al. Back then, it was uncommon for a woman to freeze her eggs 'just in case,' so that option would not have been something I would have considered at all. Thinking about what could have been has not helped my situation. However, if I had known about my potential issues, I would have been better prepared for the possible outcomes, even if it meant realising that some things were out of my control.

While I felt like a failure at the time, it was only a temporary one. Life needed to be lived again, and that's exactly what we did.

I am now in a place where it is okay to not have kids and be a mum, it took some time to get there, but I made it. Although I know this will continue to come up in the future and may impact me, I choose to focus on all the good I have in my life, and I choose to be happy.

You can too.

The pain never fully goes away, but you learn to live with it. Don't dwell on who you wanted to be in the past; look instead at the potential of what you can become. Life's challenges can turn into our greatest lessons. Historical experiences can influence how you live your life, and the past can have a hold on you – so be aware of this. You can shift this by focusing on the positive aspects of your life.

Challenges in life can be our greatest lessons.

Your life is your responsibility. What you do every day reflects what you will become. Stay optimistic. I have been and will remain optimistic, regardless of the situation.

What I learnt through my IVF journey...
1. It is okay not to be OK about it.
2. You can thrive beyond this experience.
3. You need to grieve. It is okay to grieve for something you never had, and you should.
4. Friends, family, and work colleagues are important. You need to ensure they know and help them understand what you are going through.
5. Be nice to yourself.
6. Be kind to yourself.
7. Don't beat yourself up.
8. Use the lessons and the strength that these challenges give you.
9. Own it to use it however you need to.
10. Do the pros and cons of having kids versus not having them to determine what this could mean for you.
11. Find your new normal.
12. Celebrate all the small wins along the way.
13. Play BS Lotto with the silly things people say during the process. You need to turn it into something you can control or laugh at.
14. Don't blame yourself; there is nothing wrong with you.
15. Consider how you can turn this negative experience and cycle of disappointment into something that provides value to you or others.
16. Re-shape it to turn it into a gain rather than a loss.

17. Instead of being stuck in disappointment and grief, explore new ways to discover your happiness and balance.
18. Ask for help and get support - seek whatever support you need to make it easier.
19. Start the conversation. Speak to someone. Just start talking.
20. You are not alone; speak up about it, and you will discover others facing similar experiences and expand your support network.

What I've learnt that helps me every day...
1. Create a clear purpose for your life – what are you aiming for?
2. Be kind to yourself, and don't feel bad for feeling unhappy sometimes.
3. Embrace change.
4. Surround yourself with positive and caring people.
5. Build your confidence with positive beliefs.
6. Regularly reflect on what you have, not what you don't have.
7. Find out what brings you joy and makes you smile and do it.
8. Laugh, laugh, laugh. Find the funny side in a crappy situation.
9. Be grateful for what you have every day. Don't waste it thinking about what you don't have. That's a waste of time and energy you could invest in what you enjoy or the people you love.
10. Learn something new, move, and journal most days.
11. You cannot control every outcome in your life, so you need to learn to let go.
12. Life is not always a smooth ride. You have to learn how to handle the bumps along the way.

13. You need a plan to support you on your journey, but not a rigid one. Have a 'Plan B.'
14. You need to be flexible.
15. Appreciate the 'now' and what you have and be happy and content with that.
16. Find real connections with others and discuss your challenges openly.
17. Be your authentic self.
18. Appreciate your life (you only get one) just as it is, even if it is not how you envisaged it would be.
19. You cannot control everything happening around you or what has happened to you, but you can control your response to what has happened.
20. Find your passion, what excites and energises you, and what you lose yourself in.

Finally, I learnt that my value lies in helping others, and this aligns with my purpose.

"You only live once,
but if you do it right, once is enough."
(Mae West)

Afterword

To those I know and those I don't who are experiencing something similar, reaching the end of this journey and beyond can be challenging. However, your life can still be fulfilled even if it looks different from what you had planned.

You are amazing, strong, and courageous, and **you are not alone**.

Don't dwell on who you wanted to be in the past; focus on the potential of who you can become.

Challenges in life can be our greatest lessons.

Acknowledgements

To my husband Al, my rock, soul mate, and best friend. You are a caring, loving, fun optimist who tells it how it is. Thanks for being you and for continuously bringing laughter, joy and fun into our lives, no matter how tough it gets. I cannot imagine doing life with anyone else.

Mum and Dad, you are my rocks, supporting and encouraging me in everything I do. Thank you.

To Janine, Darlene, Clinton, my in-laws, and all my nieces and nephews, thanks for all the joy, laughter and encouragement you bring. I love doing life with you all.

To my lifelong friends Jane and Jacky, thank you for your unwavering support through all of life's ups and downs. I truly appreciate the fun, laughter and craziness we share together.

Thanks to my friends in Perth for all your support and encouragement, specifically Lesley, for your valuable input and guidance while writing this book.

To our extended family and friends, thanks for being there for us when we needed it back then and when we need it now.

A heartfelt thanks to everyone who has supported and encouraged me on my journey to write this book. You all know who you are, and I genuinely appreciate having each of you in my life.

Finally, I wanted to extend a special thanks to those who shared their stories with me and contributed to this book and our life story. You are all amazing and resilient individuals. It is a privilege to have you all in our lives.

About the Author

Sharyn is an experienced senior corporate executive holding diverse roles across multiple industries. She has a warm, outgoing, and adaptable leadership style that fosters building strong, lasting relationships and connections that inspire and motivate others. She is committed to building high-performing teams and emphasises trust, communication, collaboration and flexibility in her approach. Sharyn seeks to bring balance and perspective to her leadership and strives to lead with authenticity and vulnerability in an open and transparent way.

Her dedication to mentoring and coaching others, combined with her breadth of leadership experience, contributed to her being recognised as one of the Most Inspiring Women in Commerce and Contracting in 2021.

Her focus has been on balancing her career with personal aspects of her life, including an ultimately unsuccessful IVF journey and how she leaned into a fulfilling and balanced life. She is passionate about making these taboo conversations a part of everyday discussions and creating a safe space to support people through various life phases, both personally and in the workplace.

She is a lifelong learner and an eternal optimist, regardless of the circumstance.

Connect with Sharyn if you would like to explore more on this topic. http://linkedin.com/in/sharyn-county-6b5b609

sharyncounty.com.au

References
Endnotes

1. World Health Organisation, Fertility Fact Sheet. (https://www.who.int/news-room/fact-sheets/detail/infertility) - Viewed May 2023

2. World Health Organisation (WHO). International Classification of Diseases, 11th Revision (ICD-11) Geneva: WHO 2018)

3. World Health Organisation, Infertility prevalence estimates, 1990-2021. Geneva: World Health Organization; 2023. Licence: CC BY-NC-SA 3.0 IGO

4. Dr Brene Brown, The Power of Vulnerability - Brene Brown (youtube.com) Aug 15 2013 viewed March 2023 (https://www.youtube.com/watch?v=sXSjc-pbXk4&t=0s)

5. Dr Brene Brown, The Power of Vulnerability - Brene Brown (youtube.com) Aug 15 2013 viewed March 2023 (https://www.youtube.com/watch?v=sXSjc-pbXk4&t=0s)

6. Jay Shetty, Famous Failures Part 2 (youtube.com) 5 April 2016 viewed January 2022 (https://www.youtube.com/watch?v=bAwXAFz6cmA)

7 Jack Kornfield, Buddha's Little Instruction Book, May 1, 1994 by Bantam

8 Anne Frank, The Diary of a Young Girl, July 1, 1993 by Bantam

9 Fertility Matters (https://www.fertilitymatters.org.au) - Viewed November 2023

10 Jean Hailes for Women's Health, Understanding Polycystic Ovary Syndrome All you need to know, March 2020 (https://www.jeanhailes.org.au/) Viewed April 2021

11 Polycystic Ovary Syndrome (PCOS) Merck Healthcare Pty Ltd.) Polycystic Ovary Syndrome (PCOS) (Hyperandrogenic Chronic Anovulation; Stein-Leventhal Syndrome) By JoAnn V. Pinkerton, MD, University of Virginia Health System March 2020 / Reviewed/Revised Jan 2023. - Viewed April 2021

12 Dr Alex Polyakov, Polycystic ovaries or PCOS – What's the difference? June 2015 (http://www.fertilitypharmacy.com.au/blog/Polycystic-ovaries-or-PCOS-Whats-the-difference) - Viewed April 2021

13 Better Health Channel, Polycystic Ovarian Syndrome PCOS (https://www.betterhealth.vic.gov.au/health/conditionsandtreatments/polycystic-ovarian-syndrome-pcos#bhc-content) - Viewed November 2023

14 World Health Organisation (WHO). International Classification of Diseases, 11th Revision (ICD-11) Geneva: WHO 2018)

15 World Health Organisation, Fertility Fact Sheet (https://www.who.int/news-room/fact-sheets/detail/infertility) - Viewed May 2023

REFERENCES

16 World Health Organisation, Infertility prevalence estimates, 1990-2021. Geneva: World Health Organization; 2023. Licence: CC BY-NC-SA 3.0 IGO

17 World Health Organisation Website (https://www.who.int/health-topics/infertility#tab=tab_1) - Viewed, 4 Nov, 2021

18 World Health Organisation, Infertility prevalence estimates, 1990-2021. Geneva: World Health Organization; 2023. Licence: CC BY-NC-SA 3.0 IGO

19 The Fertility Society of Australia & New Zealand Website, Understanding Infertility and getting to know your options (https://www.fertilitysociety.com.au/) - Viewed April 2023

20 United Nations Website, The Sustainable Development Agenda. (https://www.un.org/sustainabledevelopment/development-agenda) / 2023(Un.Og/sustainabledevelopment/development-agenda) - Viewed November

21 Valerie Shrimplin, Channa N. Jayasena; Was Henry VIII Infertile? Miscarriages and Male Infertility in Tudor England. The Journal of Interdisciplinary History 2021; 52 (2): 155–176. doi: (https://doi.org/10.1162/jinh_a_01695)

22 The Lancet Global Health, Vol 10, Issue 6, E778-E779, (https://www.thelancet.com/journals/langlo/article/PIIS2214-109X(22)00205-4/fulltext) – Viewed June 2022

23 World Health Organisation, Violence against women (who.int) (https://www.who.int/news-room/fact-sheets/detail/violence-against-women) - Viewed February 2024

24 Australian Bureau of Statistics Website, Partner violence, 2021-22 financial year | Australian Bureau of Statistics (abs.gov.au) (https://www.abs.gov.au/statistics/people/

crime-and-justice/partner-violence/latest-release) - Viewed February 2024

25 United Nations Population Fund Website, The Problem with too few.(https://www.unfpa.org/swp2023/too-few) - Viewed April 2023

26 Australian Bureau of Statistics Website Australian fertility rate hits record low | Australian Bureau of Statistics (abs.gov.au) https://www.abs.gov.au/media-centre/media-releases/australian-fertility-rate-hits-record-low - Viewed November 2022

27 Australian Bureau of Statistics Website , Births Australia, 2021 | Australian Bureau of Statistics (abs.gov.au) (https://www.abs.gov.au/statistics/people/population/births-australia/2021) - Viewed November 2022

28 Australian Bureau of Statistics Website, Births Australia, 2021 | Australian Bureau of Statistics (abs.gov.au)(https://www.abs.gov.au/statistics/people/population/births-australia/2021) - Viewed November 2022

29 The Fertility Society of Australia & New Zealand Website, Age and Reproductive Outcomes (https://www.yourfertility.org.au/sites/default/files/2018-11/Age_and_reproductive_outcomes.pdf - Viewed April 2023

30 The Fertility Society of Australia & New Zealand Website, Age and Reproductive Outcomes https://www.yourfertility.org.au/sites/default/files/2018-11/Age_and_reproductive_outcomes.pdf - Viewed April 2023

31 The Fertility Society of Australia & New Zealand Website, How to increase your chance of getting pregnant | Your Fertility (https://www.yourfertility.org.au/how-increase-your-chance-getting-pregnant) - Viewed May 2023.

REFERENCES

32   Creating a Family Website, How Many IVF Cycles Should You Try Before Giving Up? - Creating a Family (https://creatingafamily.org/infertility-category/how-many-ivf-cycles-should-you-try-before-giving-up/) - Viewed November 2022.

33   Wang YA, Dean JH, Grayson N & Sullivan EA 2006. Assisted reproduction technology in Australia and New Zealand 2004. Assisted reproduction technology series no. 10. Cat. no. PER 39. Sydney: AIHW National Perinatal Statistics Unit. (https://npesu.unsw.edu.au/sites/default/files/npesu/data_collection/Assisted%20reproductive%20technology%20in%20Australia%20and%20New%20Zealand%202004.pdf)

34   Newman JE, Kotevski DP, Paul RC, Chambers GM 2024. Assisted reproductive technology in Australia and New Zealand 2022. Sydney: National Perinatal Epidemiology and Statistics Unit, the University of New South Wales, Sydney. (https://www.unsw.edu.au/content/dam/pdfs/research/2024-09-npesu/2024-09-assisted-reproductive-technology-in-australia-and-new-zealand-2022.pdf)

35   Dow K. Looking into the Test Tube: The Birth of IVF on British Television. Med Hist. 2019 Apr;63(2):189-208. doi: 10.1017/mdh.2019.6. PMID: 30912501; PMCID: PMC6434648.(https://www.ncbi.nlm.nih.gov/pmc/articles/PMC6434648/#:~:text=The%20birth%20of%20the%20world's,of%20technologically%20assisted%20human%20reproduction.) - Viewed November 2022

36   Victorian Assisted Reproductive Treatment Authority Website, History of donor conception | VARTA (https://www.varta.org.au/about/projects/history-donor-conception) - Viewed November 2022

[37] Your IVF Success Website, Understanding IVF(https://yourivfsuccess.com.au/understanding-ivf) - Viewed November 2023

[38] Dean JH and Sullivan EA 2003. Assisted conception Australia and New Zealand 2000 and 2001. AIHW Cat. No. PER 22. Sydney: Australian Institute of Health and Welfare National Perinatal Statistics Unit (Assisted Conception Series No. 7). (https://npesu.unsw.edu.au/sites/default/files/npesu/data_collection/Assisted%20conception%20Australia%20and%20New%20Zealand%202000%20and%202001.pdf)

[39] Newman JE, Paul RC, Chambers GM 2023. Assisted reproductive technology in Australia and New Zealand 2021. Sydney: National Perinatal Epidemiology and Statistics Unit, the University of New South Wales, Sydney. (https://npesu.unsw.edu.au/sites/default/files/npesu/data_collection/Assisted%20Reproductive%20Technology%20in%20Australia%20and%20New%20Zealand%202021.pdf (Assisted Reproductive Database (ANZARD))

[40] The Fertility Society of Australia & New Zealand Website, Age and Reproductive Outcomes (https://www.yourfertility.org.au/sites/default/files/2018-11/Age_and_reproductive_outcomes.pdf) - Viewed April 2023

[41] Money Creating Financial Freedom Website (https://www.moneymag.com.au/cost-of-ivf) - Viewed May 2022.

[42] Forbes Health Website, How Much Does IVF Cost In 2024? – Forbes Health (https://www.forbes.com/health/womens-health/how-much-does-ivf-cost/) Viewed November 2023

REFERENCES

43 Di Guardo F, Pluchino N, Drakopoulos P. Treatment modalities for poor ovarian responders. Ther Adv Reprod Health. 2023 Jan 24;17:26334941221147464. doi: 10.1177/26334941221147464. PMID: 36713768; PMCID: PMC9880576. (https://www.ncbi.nlm.nih.gov/pmc/articles/PMC9880576/)

44 J.F. Oudendijk, F. Yarde, M.J.C. Eijkemans, F.J.M. Broekmans, S.L. Broer, The poor responder in IVF: is the prognosis always poor? A systematic review, Human Reproduction Update, Volume 18, Issue 1, January/February 2012, Pages 1–11, (https://doi.org/10.1093/humupd/dmr037)

45 Commonwealth of Australia 2021 Australian Institute of Family Studies, Families in Australia Survey Towards Covid Normal Report np.4 Impacts of Covid-19 on pregnancy and fertility intentions July 2021. (https://static.aifs.gov.au/files/sgBtyhAerg/2106_4_FIAS_pregnancy_and_fertility_intentions.pdf?_ga=2.164680890.443463432.1672719299-1498368441.1672719298)

46 Australian Bureau of Statistics Website Australian fertility rate hits record low | Australian Bureau of Statistics (abs.gov.au) (https://www.abs.gov.au/media-centre/media-releases/australian-fertility-rate-hits-record-low) - Viewed November 2022.

47 World Health Organisation, Infertility prevalence estimates, 1990-2021. Geneva: World Health Organization; 2023. Licence: CC BY-NC-SA 3.0 IGO.

48 Patel, Ansha; Sharma, P. S. V. N.; Kumar, Pratap1,2; Binu, V. S.3.Illness Cognitions, Anxiety, and Depression in Men and Women Undergoing Fertility Treatments: A Dyadic Approach. Journal of Human Reproductive Sciences 11(2):p

180-189, Apr–Jun 2018. | DOI: 10.4103/jhrs.JHRS_119_17 (https://journals.lww.com/jhrs/fulltext/2018/11020/illness_cognitions,_anxiety,_and_depression_in_men.17.aspx)

49 Fertility matters at work Survey Results 2020 C. Ingle, B. Kearns, N. Silverman, (April 2020), Fertility Matters at Work Survey 2020. (https://fertilitymattersatwork.com/resource-library/) – Viewed April 2020

50 MIST Workshops Ltd https://www.mistworkshops.com/ - Viewed May 2024.

51 Schnitzler, K.(2024), "The Intersect of Miscarriage and Work: Concealment, Minimization and Discriminatory Practice", Wilkinson, K. and Woolnough, H. (Ed.) Work-Life Inclusion: Broadening Perspectives Across the Life-Course, Emerald Publishing Limited, Leeds, pp. 81-94. (https://doi.org/10.1108/978-1-80382-219-820241007)

52 Dr K Wilkinson, Dr. C Mumford, Dr M Caroll, (May 2022) Manchester Metropolitan University, Complex Fertility Journeys and Employment, How workers navigate fertility challenges, including fertility treatment, alongside work and employment, and what employers can do to help.

53 Serena G. Sohrab and Nada Basir Nov 11 2020 Harvard Business Review Website "Employers, It's Time to Talk About Infertility" () (https://hbr.org/2020/11/employers-its-time-to-talk-about-infertility.) - Viewed January 2022.

Notes

WHAT NOW... I DON'T HAVE KIDS!

NOTES

www.ingramcontent.com/pod-product-compliance
Lightning Source LLC
Chambersburg PA
CBHW061230070526
44584CB00030B/4064